# The Hummingbird Prophecy

*For anyone who has encountered suicide*

Lorijane Graham

Produced by Scottsdale Multimedia, Inc.

Cover design by Leslie Ann Kekuewa

ISBN: 146354121X
ISBN-13: 9781463541217

LCCN:

**Dedicated to the loving memory of**

**Michaela Lynn Wegner**
**1989-2005**

# ACKNOWLEDGMENTS

John Bingham, John Brockmeyer, James L. Thompson, Leslie Ann Kekuewa, Peter Lipresti, Tom DeWitt, Tanya Farouki, Wendy Francis, Niki McNamara, Ginny Moynahan, Lynda James, Elmer Hata and Emma James. Special thanks to Bill.

# Prologue

I look out of my bedroom window to the upscale, suburban street below. Its a pretty picture of the neighborhood edging toward summer: manicured lawns, sweeping driveways, red brick and white siding. The eyebrows of dormer windows pop up from roofs here and there to take a look around. It all appears like a postcard, like perfection caught on paper.

But for me, it's a postcard from a place where I don't live anymore. Even though I stand here with my feet planted in the carpet of my family home, my eyes open to the scene, I do not feel I belong in this familiar place. I wonder if I am actually present in this ghost of a world, or if the world alone exists, with me a ghost within it.

As I watch, the postcard attempts to prove itself real by lurching into motion. A car backs out and heads toward the city. The noise of a lawn mower buzzes somewhere to the right. A mother and two children emerge from a minivan and ring a doorbell, probably right on time for their weekly play date.

I look at the clock. It's 10:30 a.m., and this is what would normally be taking place at 10:30 a.m. The mail will be delivered. The daytime TV schedule will be the same as always. Eventually, kids will emerge from buses, and parents come home from work.

I look at my hands and think, *How do they not know? How can this day -- any day from here on -- be the same as the time before?*

Before. Before the tragedy. Before the loss of my daughter.

*No*, I correct myself. *Before the **theft** of my daughter.*

The world around me continues somehow, and I sit as at the center of the spinning compass, dizzy. I had tried at first to prop myself up by getting back on the merry-go-round. I climbed forcefully into the daily schedule and used the everyday routine as a crutch, a way of marking time and forcing it to pass.

People do it all the time.

But it's impossible to explain to someone who hasn't experienced such intense loss how the so-called real world is not as real as most people take for granted, that everyday reality is just a mask. Unless you have known firsthand the aftermath of an emotional catastrophe, you cannot know that the inside of your mind is also a physical place, more solid and real than the smiling faces of neighbors or the television news or even the changeable weather. More real than the groceries in the refrigerator or the traffic of the morning commute.

The mind is a warm place, soft and comforting. It offers definable walls, to keep you in and other things away. Tight and sticky, it's also hard to re-emerge once you enter the space of your own mind, with its unstoppable thoughts and surges of intense emotion.

They keep bringing me food and flowers. They keep telling me it will all be okay. One day, some day, it will be all right. They tell me she is in a better place.

*A better place? Wouldn't anywhere be better than here?*

I close the blinds, turn on the television for background noise and submerge myself again in the bedding. I breathe in the musty but soft scent of the pillows. From deep inside my physical self, where the real me is curled up in pain, she weeps and wails: "They all leave you. They all intentionally and violently leave you. Everyone is in this better place but you."

*Then why shouldn't I go, too?*

I listen with my ears, with my skin, with my mind, but there is yet no answer.

## Chapter One

Like my mother and father before me, I grew up in Blackstone, Massachusetts. Located in the extreme south of the state, we sat just miles north of the Rhode Island border and the town of Woonsocket. As is typically said about small towns, you knew everybody and everybody knew you, though at the time there were more than 5,000 residents.

In so many other ways, it was also a typical New England town. The Blackstone River, wide and strong enough to power industry, brought the first textile mill to the region in the early 1800s, and it was followed by others, creating a need for our little hamlet in the area. There was a quaint main street with narrow roads and shops all named after the town: the Blackstone Potato Chip Factory, the Blackstone Garage, and so on. There was an old railroad station, and further along, small older homes that once housed railroad workers, and the larger bungalows of the white-collar families.

All throughout there was that standard New England vegetation, growing strong through every patch of dirt or crack of sidewalk. Lush and moist, you couldn't keep back the limber trees, curling vines, wildflowers and grasses, the latter growing faster than you could mow, it seemed. And then there was the riot of color in the fall, the autumn colors infusing the town with red and gold and yellow for a few weeks each year.

Every yard had a little bit of wildness about it. Most kids had at least a little patch of forest to play in.

Most of the adults had a very industrial job to support them. During my youth in the 1960s, the age of the textile mills and railroads was setting. Blackstone's residents were instead working for a local mills or factories, or more notably, the recently founded Tupperware factory. Truckloads and railcar loads of raw materials in the form of clear plastic pellets arrived for the factory regularly. They were maybe a quarter of an inch in diameter. We kids would find the little pellets in gutters and ditches. Sometimes the more enterprising would find ways to steal handfuls, stuffed in pockets or cradled in shirtfronts, to bring home for various games or crafts.

It was not an area that had weathered The Great Depression well, the era in which my father, Frank Dubois, and my mother, Joan Dubois, grew up.

My father's family was always a bit of a mystery to me. I know that times were hard financially, which might have been why he left school early. Then again, he might have up and quit simply because he was rebellious and craved freedom, and his innate ability with machines could provide him with a job and an income even when he was still really just a teen. Therefore, he left home quite early.

It perhaps wasn't obvious to outsiders that Dad was not as well educated as most. His speech and manner were normal, aside from the heavy New England accent and a propensity for mild curses. I don't think his vocabulary was very large, so he just stuck in a few curse words whenever he couldn't think of a better word. He was almost six feet tall and hovered around 185 pounds, large enough to be imposing to many people, but he had the lightest touch as a mechanic. While numbers and letters didn't filter through his head very well, any machinery made sense to his eye. It seemed he could map an engine or transmission repair in his head, taking it apart, diagnosing the problem, and putting it back together again all in his mind. But beyond signing his name on documents, he couldn't understand complicated things very well and didn't seem to want to learn, getting by just fine as he did. With dark hair, sideburns and a slightly impish smirk, he was quite devil-may-care and mischievous by nature.

My father had two older sisters, Nancy and Gert. Nancy's name had always been cloaked in some mysterious scandal surrounding her second husband, who resided in town. Gert had married a tubby, jolly man named Roberto and lived in downtown Blackstone, where she leathered her skin with excessive sunbathing and chain smoking. Dad would take us kids to go visit only occasionally and only if we swore not to leak news of the clandestine encounter to our mother, alluding to but never explaining some angry rift between the families. Even so, I knew that when my bike chain fell off while I was in town, Uncle Roberto would be more than happy to get his chubby fingers greasy and help me fix it, waving as I rode off home, where I guess he knew he would never be welcome.

Instead of getting to know my father's family and past, my childhood was enveloped with the presence, conversation and smells -- either feminine perfume or cigarette smoke -- of my mother's large brood, the Camerons.

She'd pointed out to me several times the home she and the family grew up in on Bridge Street in the part of Blackstone known as Waterford. In the mid 19th Century, a textile factory called Red Mill brought a lot of Irish workers to the area, many of whom came from the town of Waterford in their native land. So the name came either from that or because the neighborhood was located right on the water, but the locally influential and well known St. Paul's Catholic Church might point toward the former.

By the 1920s and 30s, those workers' homes were struggling, to say the least, and my mother's family was no exception. She told me of those hard times in little drips and dabs, but never the complete story. Instead, one time as we walked by she pointed at the little postage stamp yard, overgrown with vegetation. "Some of my brothers and sisters are buried in that yard," she said dispassionately. "Mother sometimes came to her time and had them on the kitchen floor." She pointed toward one of the home's windows. "And they seemed to like as not be stillborn. So we kids would have to find a shoebox and were told to bury them in the backyard." When I asked how they died she said a variety of reasons but one that sticks out in my mind was a baby that died of boils. I couldn't understand why a child would die of such a thing but I guess they are infections and if you have multiple boils and you are young and weak you could die from them.

My mother had told me that had they all lived, there would have been at least 11 Cameron children. Instead, the surviving nine buried the unlucky two.

She seemed quite nonplussed, as if in dropping that piece of history she wasn't letting me get to know her better or teaching me to enjoy a fleeting and precious life. She wanted to prove that she'd been there and done that. And if she'd done that, well then . . . nothing I had to complain about in my privileged little childhood mattered, did it?

As for my mother's living family, there were the dead brothers, my uncles Mike and Danny, killed in one of the wars, which we occasionally visited at the cemetery to leave flowers and clean up their gravesites when it was our turn, all very brisk and business-like.

There wasn't a lot of sentimentality in that branch of the family, I learned early on, bonded by blood but not genuine affection as they were. No use complaining about your own bad circumstances, because turn to your right and someone else can complain long and loud about how they've had it worse.

My maternal grandmother was Emma, who lived down in Woonsocket in a small apartment. Out of familial duty, the kids took turns helping her clean her place once a year, and it was not a pleasant grandmotherly experience. The walls were yellow and even brown in places thanks to tobacco smoke, hanging there like an extra layer of blown-on wallpaper. Near the kitchen where cooking grease coated the walls, the smoke and ash would stick like fly paper, and you could write your name in it with your finger tip, revealing the original paint color beneath. She died when I was so young that I never remember her healthy and hale, only frail and sickly, even when she ventured from her television-loud, smoke-filled home to our house to play canasta with my mother and the other girls.

Except for two of the sisters -- Aunt Sandra died soon after I was born, and Aunt Roz lived in another town -- the family canasta game was one of their favorite pursuits and took place around our kitchen table. Cards of that sort were apparently a female occupation, as neither my father nor my Uncle Jack would dare to stick their noses into the game. I would hide underneath the table, making it my little tent, and stare at all their bulgy, bony and otherwise misshapen knees as they played.

The women of the family seemed to come in two variations: large and wide, and tiny and square. Vicky, who had been in the Army, was both tall and stout with legs like tree trunks; Carley was built similar, and was known to go outside with my father to smoke with him. Emma was my favorite. She was small and slender and, at least in terms of her personality, quite soft and gentle, uncharacteristic for one of this clan. She allowed me to pillow my head on her cardiganed shoulder. Mother was also small, maybe 4 foot 11 inches at the most, but with a strong jaw and shoulders that visually connected her and smaller Emma with the larger ladies, showing they were all cut from the same cloth.

And I sat beneath there, the sun and their cigarette smoke filtered through the tablecloth, and looked at the odd collection of knees, packed together like a hideous herd of beasts at a watering trough. Some were large, with blunt right angles, and some knobby and small as a larger woman's arm. One of my favorite things to do in those days was to play with all of the loose skin on my grandmother's arms and legs. She must have been heavier before and the loose baggy skin that hung under her arms was both disgusting and peculiar and my fascination with flipping it about with my hands annoyed her more than anything. It was fun to "get her" and try to avoid the swat that naturally followed. Under her biceps was so much skin it looked like an elephant ear.

Unlike my father and despite her meager family, my mother had been able to complete high school and wasn't about to let anybody forget it, including my father. She stood almost a foot shorter than him, but that strong attitude set in stone put him in his place, using big vocabulary words that she knew would confound him. She may have been birdlike in stature, but she seemed to carry strength of will in her bones and joints. Pale with dark eyes, she wore her black hair bobbed at ear level. She plucked her eyebrows to the point that they were almost nonexistent and wore thick coats of red lipstick. Her clothes, on the other hand, were always unremarkable. The vast majority of the time she was wearing some sort of plain dress covered by a plain house apron.

To this day, I do not know where or how my parents met, what attracted them to one another or the circumstances of their marriage. I have only the photo taken on the day of their wedding, which must have been small and relatively informal, because the wedding dress wasn't fancy and the tux my dad wore was of the inexpensive type for that time. There's only a staged picture, the type where you go into a studio to pose and the photographer tells you to tilt your chin to the right and smile a little wider, then snaps a few different angles. Probably because of the vast height difference, my mother is seated in the photo. My father stands behind. To me, she seems the same, but his hair is lighter brown and curly, very debonair.

*

Lorijane Graham, that's me. I was born in 1962, making me Joan and Dad's fourth child out of five.

When I got to the age where a child actually begins to remember her life -- for me, that was about four years old -- my two older sisters had already left childhood behind to begin their own families. My sister Hope was 11 years older than me, and Chris was 10 years my senior. They'd been the first wave of our parents' brood, there being 8 years after Chris until my brother Mike showed up, two more for me and then five more years for the final act, my youngest sister Michelle. That I know of, no one can account for the 11-year gap. It sits there in the unexplained, neatly separating the siblings into the older and younger groups.

It's a fairly easy distinction for me, because the two groups rarely lived together under the same roof. My older sisters lived a relatively short time with us in the house that I consider my childhood home, a saltbox colonial on Blackstone Street, north of the river. They were soon off on their own, Hope to be married soon thereafter, and I remember their children as much as I remember my sisters themselves.

The saltbox colonial was white and two stories tall, set back from the street by the distance of a good-sized front yard with a line of mature trees down the right-hand side. There was a fence around flower beds near the home's foundation and an imbedded boulder that we melted crayons on in the summer. From the road, it was shaped exactly like a box with a flat front and a slanted roof down the back. The door was placed front and center, while black-shuttered windows flanked each side and ran in a neat line along the upper level. It was a solidly middle class home, and no one could say the white edifice wasn't downright respectable.

The neighborhood was what I would call mixed. There were certainly homes that were bigger than ours, some with their own pools and classic white picket fences. Then not far away, some families lived in trailer homes that seemed more and more permanent and the grass and weeds grew up the walls. The house across the street was actually a converted tavern where the owners had cleared out the basement for living space. Everyone said it would make a great bomb shelter.

We moved into Blackstone Street when the home was still new. The upper level was complete but unfinished, with bare board floors and plywood walls, waiting for carpet and plaster. It felt as if someone else had bought it, or almost bought it, then changed their minds. Mike and I lived in the two bedrooms upstairs -- both of which had a door to a storage area in the back -- with a bath my parents added on sandwiched between my space and my brother's. For a while, it was half done and there were only temporary cardboard walls for privacy in between. Hope's husband Philip was quite handy with carpentry and worked on completing the upstairs. I think the motivation was their need to live with us for a while after they were married. The project was long and noisy and once it was finished, the upstairs had a rather rustic, almost "log cabin" look to it.

Downstairs there was my parents' room, both a living room and a family room, an average sized kitchen, floored in a mixture of orange and brown linoleum, light toned hardwood and carpet. The kitchen had dark cabinets and old-fashioned, white lace curtains hung cafe style. Of my parents' room, I remember only the large bed with its heavy headboard of light wood.

The basement was unfinished, with concrete floors. The laundry, a refrigerator and (for some reason) a honky-tonk piano took up some space, but the rest could be used as a roller skating rink when we felt like it, the wheels churning up thin, gray concrete dust. The emergency brake when you got going too fast was the big, imposing black oil tank for the house's heating system. When it was being filled and I was downstairs, I was fascinated by the glugging sound of the tank replenishing all that liquid that kept us warm through the winter. When my mother hung the laundry to dry down in the basement during the cold months, the roller skating would become more acrobatic as I dove and dodged under the stiff jeans, T-shirts and underwear.

Outside the house we had a significant amount of yard for us kids to play and our father to work. Dad quickly built his garage, though whether from scratch or by improving a structure that was already there, I don't know. In addition to the numerous jobs he held at Hannora Mills, Guillmond Farms and Garelick Farms Dairy, Dad had a pretty brisk business buying, fixing and selling vehicles and vehicle parts of all makes and models.

The garage sat down a gently sloping hill from the back of the house, within shouting distance, but only if you put some *oomph* into it. He poured a concrete slab in front of the garage next to a massive oak tree, and he'd rigged up a pulley system from one of its thick and flexing branches to lift motors and other large objects. He called this the chain fall.

For us kids, there was a metal swing set prone to rust, and a tire swing that Dad had hung for us.

As time went by the land around the house became both a parking lot and a junkyard. Vehicles that could not be fixed, either because they'd reached the end of the road or their owner couldn't afford to foot the repairs, sunk incrementally into the dirt and grew grass between their tire treads. Parts of all sorts had been flung wherever they might land, my father's playful and haphazard form of organization that made finding a particular item like a scavenger hunt.

In the upper backyard directly behind the house we'd hold family get-togethers after church or on holidays like the Fourth of July. My mother's siblings, all my cousins and my sisters' families would be in attendance, as such large Catholic families expect and require.

My sister Michelle, five years my junior, was soon born. In one distinct memory of her as a baby I remember that because I was still very small and young, I was placed in a sturdy chair before they handed me Michelle to hold on one leg, cradled in one arm. One of my older sister's babies was placed on the other leg, secured by the other arm. Both babies together came up to my chin and overflowed my lap. I was very excited and confused at the time that one baby was the other baby's aunt, the other baby the niece. My aunts were all old and towering, intimidating -- nothing like a little baby -- and this news seemed too strange to be believed.

Another time while my sisters were visiting I recall being in the bath with little Michelle. Someone must have stepped away for a moment as the door was ajar and there were adult voices on the other side. The memory is just a snippet, mostly the feeling of how slippery my little sister was. The touch of her skin, just like mine, made me think on the fact that she was not a doll. She was human and a girl just like me, just smaller and more fragile. I had to take care of her.

Every Sunday we would get dressed up in our best for church, St. Paul's, which stood one half in North Smithfield and one half in Blackstone. St. Paul's was where I went to school every day, catechism on Wednesdays and confession on Fridays, as well as church on Sundays. Mike and I would have to stand very politely and still, either by the front door or outside by the car waiting until all family members were ready and prepared to leave because our mother didn't trust us not to run off into the woods or trip or spill or otherwise muss our clothing and hair, which had been styled specifically to impress the priest and other church-going families. I'd cross my white-gloved hands in front of my frilly dress, so my mother wouldn't think I was going to touch anything and remind, "Don't you dare get those dirty." Dad would stand by the car door and wait, smoking a final cigarette, looking at his watch every five minutes.

We'd get in the car and make the drive, eventually joining all the others streaming into the big stone church for the service, one of the oldest and largest buildings that wasn't a factory in the area. We were told to smile, even if we didn't feel like it, and we waved to my mom's family and ignored my dad's sisters, even though some of them also attended St. Paul's. My father would often fall asleep and snore, woken by my mother's pointed whispers of, "Cut. It. Out."

Sunday afternoons, Mike and I found it best to not hang around the house but to get outdoors, though usually on our separate pursuits and not together. Being gone five days a week to school, this is what our mother was used to and expected. She didn't like us underfoot, and didn't like us hovering (or even what she felt was hovering). She often thought we were in her way or found we tried her nerves, even in silence.

But we were expected home by five p.m. On the dot. She may not have been a wonderful cook -- in fact, the food was awful -- but that's when dinner was on the table and the children were expected. The dinners worked on a strict schedule, most things with my mother being strict. Mondays brought leftovers. Tuesday was steak or liver, usually pan-fried and difficult to chew. Then we cycled through spaghetti Wednesdays, goulash Thursdays, fish for Fridays, of course, and "fend for yourself" dinner on Saturdays. Even outside of dinners, the rest of the food wasn't tasty either. My father brought home the milk from the dairy he worked at, and it was always slightly sour. My older sister Hope worked at a bakery, so our baked goods were dry cookies but the raisins made them feel moist and 3 day old bread.

But Sunday? Sunday was corned beef and cabbage. I hated the cabbage. It made the whole house smell and the texture was like slug skin, but it was how things had always been done, and how things would always continue to be done as far as my strict and stringent mother was concerned.

If I arrived home at 5:02 -- because I wasn't wearing my Sunday best, because no strangers were around, because we had no other family in the house -- my mother would get angry. When she was angry, her cheeks flamed red and her tiny stride became a violent stomp.

"What do you think you're doing being late?" she'd yell, her eyes flaring wide on the word *late*.

Then her diminutive hand, with the strength of her anger and wiry muscles, would strike me flat-palmed across the face, crushing my nose to one side. She'd follow through completely with the stroke, her hand winding up poised above her opposite shoulder.

And then (this was one of her other family rules, much like the five p.m. dinner curfew) if the nose refused to bleed with one blow, the hand would descend again, swinging down the other direction to backhand my face, the nose crunching in the other direction. In other words, there had to be blood before she was satisfied that punishment had been meted out sufficiently. And in my experience, the nose is a part of the body that is happy to comply, gushing with blood when it did choose to bleed.

Mother would then take a dishtowel off a nearby counter or from the strings of her apron, hand it to me, and say, "Now clean up your bloody mess. And be on time next time."

## Chapter Two

On the surface of things we appeared to be a completely normal family. Even beneath that veneer of normalcy put on for others, I didn't think anything was too abnormal, not having known anything else.

As a child, abuse was simply part of the way life was, as ordinary as brushing your hair or tying your shoes. Part of growing up is learning how to navigate the world, usually through the lessons of cause and effect. If you say please and thank you, you're more likely to get what you want. If you hit your brother, he'll likely hit you back. If you eat your vegetables, you can leave the dinner table.

But in our family home, by far and away the cause-and-effect lessons that dominated our childhood were negative reinforcement.

Joan -- which is what I prefer to call my mother -- was a late riser and didn't want to be woken before nine in the morning on weekends. The children's bedrooms being upstairs, directly above her own, she was able to hear any movement or even loud whispering before the appointed hour, and her standard reaction was to storm up the stairs.

For Mike, with his short buzzed haircut, she'd grab him by the ear; for me it was my hair, clutched in her tiny claw, clumps sandwiched between her knuckles. She would pull us bodily crashing down the stairs behind her. I remember the lip of each stair sliding under my rear end with a rhythmic thump, thump, thump. Then the screen door would screech open and I'd find myself sprawled on the grass outside the kitchen door, which faced the backyard. It was usually dewy and damp, and soaked through your pajamas in seconds. Sometimes she was a little more empathetic and would just dump us on the couch with a stern command not to make a sound.

Mike and I had developed all sorts of surreptitious routes in and out of and around the house to avoid Joan, because proximity was another cause of her flying into a rage. Even in what was then a larger house, a family tends to tread on one another's feet. But Joan seemed to have a built-in sonar system, because she could sense when a child was one inch inside her comfort zone and would immediately and lethally lash out.

Most often, Joan's first punishment instinct was the strap, which was administered onto bare buttocks with a strong and precise flick of her wrist while I was bent over the bed in my parent's bedroom. The strap was a section of a leather belt the end somewhat pointed and the holes for the belt clasp present. The leather was maybe an eighth of an inch thick and had been used often enough that it was able to bend and recover for the next blow quite quickly. Eight to ten hard strikes across the bare skin was normal but if you screamed or tried to move it would be more. The welts would be raised and purple and I remember trying to see if the imprint of the holes in the leather would also appear. Every once in a while the strap would strike the same place two or three times causing the welt to ooze blood. I can only imagine what she felt as she handed out the punishment. Sometimes I think she was convinced it would actually remove the evil in us whether real or imagined, if she hit harder and harder and longer and longer. It was always on the bare skin and the sting was intense. For that one reason I hated going into their room, averting my eyes as I went past their door. Occasionally I would be sent to the corner to kneel. Kneeling and not sitting on the heels of my feet became torture. My knees would grind and crack from the prolonged position and the linoleum over plywood floor was not very forgiving. My muscles would ache trying to keep from sitting back and her eye would catch any slouching. “Another 5 minutes!” she would yell if I made a peep or slacked in my posture even a little.

If I happened to skim by too close in a hallway, Joan would simply grab my upper arm with one hand, squeeze with the grip of a weightlifter and shake me, rattling my teeth. If I turned a corner to find myself in her path, the standard slap and often the subsequent backslap might be the punishment. In addition to cleaning up my own spilt blood, black eyes were also a common result of daily life in the Dubois house.

As a result, I always felt there was supposed to be a buffer of space around Joan, an invisible electric fence that I knew caused me only pain if I wandered too close. Like a child who learns that when you touch a hot stove, it burns, I did not even come near my mother whenever possible, let alone attempt to touch her. That action would have been so far inside her concrete barrier as to be unthinkable. What most families would consider natural and healthy hugging, cuddling or even the throwing of an arm around a shoulder were anathema to her.

The house and most things in it were also Joan's and under Joan's control, and she believed that her children were constantly scheming to steal, break or move everything. Books and magazines, potato chips and cookies, pocket change; her mind thought our hands were all over the place, up to no good. Like most children, I'm sure we did pilfer an extra cookie or dime once or twice, but nowhere near as often as we got physically punished.

Space, order and cleanliness. I may not have realized at the time, but that's what Joan demanded. Unrealistic amounts of space, order and cleanliness. She was definitely obsessive and she was certainly compulsive, too, but as I far as I know she'd never gotten a psychiatric diagnosis of any sort. I think a doctor today would have pegged her as OCD without hesitation. She just hated any form of disorder and dirt.

That's likely why I knew (I wasn't taught, but had just known from as far back as I can remember) that no foul smells of any kind were allowed within the home's walls. If I happened to get sick to my stomach, like most kids do pretty regularly, the worst thing to do would be to throw up inside the house. Doing it on the carpet or in your bed was despicable and would get your rear end spanked with Joan's paddle (an oar-shaped paddle of wood she'd picked up when the family drove through New Hampshire, ruining an otherwise pleasant memory of a mini family vacation). Much like when my nose bled, I would have to clean up my own bodily fluids and get the bedding washed as quickly as possible if I did happen to throw up in it. That is something I just didn’t understand -- if I throw up I’m obviously sick. Why get angry or lash out at me because I’m sick? What exactly did I do wrong? These were the unfathomable questions of my young mind, never quite understanding the inequities of a juvenile life.

Shooting for the trash can when you had to throw up was better. You still had to hustle the vomit outside to dump the mess and then somehow hide the smell, because she had a hunting hound's nose for bodily fluids. Even better was just swallowing it down, holding your stomach and stumbling outside, where you could vomit anywhere outside a 20 foot radius of the house without any fear of punishment.

The same procedure often went for excrement, as well. Though we had two, modern, perfectly wonderful bathrooms, if you had business to do that was going to leave behind a scent, you could not perform that business where Joan could stumble across its smell. Therefore, I was accustomed to pooping in the woods around house most of the time, here and there and wherever. My dad would light a match to mask the smell before he flushed and flush the match down so it wouldn't be in the trash can. Mike would just stay in the bathroom as long as he could hoping the stench would leave before he had to open the door. He actually developed a little bathroom game where he would make noises while on the toilet like he was driving an 18 wheel tractor and shifting it as he drove. Sometimes it was funny to listen to but other times if you were waiting to go it wasn't.

Children were just wrong, always evil and dirty and in need of punishment, according to Joan. That's the message I took away from the pain my mother dealt us on a daily basis. She made it very clear that she thought every step she took was absolutely necessary as a parent. And though many parents of the day subscribed to the school of "spare the rod and spoil the child," Joan took matters a few steps further than anyone could deem socially (or legally) acceptable.

Alum, for instance wad a powdered mineral that was used in baking and pickling, a little dab of alum was also beneficial in the treatment of mouth wounds, such as canker sores and cuts from when you'd bite your cheek or tongue. Certainly, it would sting like crazy for a little while, but that little bit could make sure the wound healed by the next morning. But if I talked back to Joan or "gave her mouth" or "gave her lip," the alum was more copiously applied.

Grabbing both my wrists in one hand, she'd lock them behind my back. Then with her fierce and bony thumb and forefinger she pried open my jaw and liberally coated the inside of my mouth with the foul powder.

It's a hard sensation to describe. Alum feels both dry -- like your mouth desperately needs water -- and acidic, burning and stinging. My eyes would water and my chin automatically thrust toward the ceiling, trying to stop both my swallowing and gag reflexes. My mouth would start to water, but because I didn't want to ingest the burning alum, drool would roll down my face. I'd try to spit out what I could, thrusting it out with my tongue to fall down the front of my shirt.

Similarly, when we said a bad word, the procedure was repeated with lava soap. She'd cut a chunk off the bar of soap and put it in my mouth. While it didn't sting as badly as the alum did, the soap got slippery with your saliva. If you weren't careful, you'd swallow the chunk of soap whole and that would make you throw up, and even more punishment could result from your punishment.

*

I often say "we" were punished, rather than using just "I." And that's because all of my siblings experienced similar abuse at one time or another, for various offenses, real or imagined.

My sister Hope, for instance, had very visible scar tissue beginning under ear, running along her shoulder and continuing down to the wrist on that side of her body. Even clothed it peaked out from the collar or her shirt or dress, and it looked like her flesh had melted and then reformed. It wasn't smooth under the touch of my small fingers.
"Where did you get your bumpy skin?" I would ask her.
"Never mind that," she said, tugging at her clothing to hide more of the scar.
"But I want to know where you got your bumpy skin."

"But you won't know, though, will you?" She would force a tense smile to make it light hearted, but it was obvious she didn't want to talk about it.

I found out years later that our mother had been boiling something in a saucepan on the stove and for some reason -- I was only able to find out the source of the scar, not the source of the disagreement -- she supposedly tossed the boiling water on her daughter, coating one side of her body with severe burns that disfigured her skin for life. That's what I was told, but I was also told she was young and reached up to grab the pot and it tipped onto her. I find the latter hard to believe since Hope was tall and would have had to be lower than the stovetop for that to happen. Whatever the truth is I know how just a simple question or remark would send Joan into instant rage and she often swatted, threw or swung at whatever was in her path.

Mike and I were the only two kids at home for the first few years that I remember, but that doesn't mean we were close. In fact, I thought of him as more than a bit strange. Given the gift of a chemistry set, he set himself about trying to blow things up. He set up a whole mini laboratory in the storage area behind his room, where he would perform "experiments" with chemicals, beakers and fire. He would take a magnifying glass and burn ants or daddy longlegs spiders on the sidewalk. He was great on a skateboard and used it as his preferred means of transportation. Mike thought of himself as supreme and intelligent beyond the comprehension of the proletarian family in which he had been born. I thought he was odd and cruel.

I had friends in the neighborhood, which had enough kids to ensure there was always someone with whom you could get into mischief. A huge chestnut tree down the street dropped its nuts to provide us with ammunition, craft supplies or other chestnut toys.

We used clothespins to attach playing cards to the spokes of our bikes to make them louder, and therefore more cool. We also tied little objects to the sissy bars of our bikes, trophies that we'd won in games of jacks, marbles and chestnuts.

But I also remember playing alone in the woods. I had found an interesting spot where four trees grew closely together and soon enough created my own club house by erecting walls between the trunks. My biggest thrill was hanging a sign on the door that read, "NO BOYS ALLOWED," and keeping my house neat and tidy and swept. My brother and one of his friends found out about the clubhouse somehow, and one day they declared war. After they tracked me down they wrestled me to the ground, held me to a tree and took turns urinating on me.

I ran home to tell Joan, but she simply said, "Well, what were you doing playing in the woods with those boys, then?" And I got in trouble and was punished for being dirty and smelly with their urine in the house.

Mike was cruel to me in many others ways. When we were playing board games he would sometimes get mad, grab my hand and squeeze it with all his might. "If you cry out, I'll just get you in trouble with Mom," he'd whisper.

Then there was the "game" of tickling. Well, everyone else who saw -- because he did it openly -- probably thought it was a game, including the adults. Just a big brother tickling his little sister. Mike would get me on the ground and tickle me, digging his fingers into my ribs so hard it sometimes left bruises. But the tickle reflex being what it is, my laughing was automatic. I couldn't stop it, no matter how hard I hated what was going on.

His face hung over me with a grin (a sneer, or smirk really) like a sick clown, and I had nightmares about Mike tickling me for years, the feeling of powerlessness and the betrayal of your own body to cry out, to stop it.

Having only two available bedrooms for the children, there was Mike's room and the girls' room. He was frustrated that I would sometimes go into his room, and I admit I did. He being bigger and stronger, it was one of the only things I could do to get back at him in any way.

However, one afternoon he set up a booby trap for me. He strung up a heavy, cast iron figurine of a greyhound dog from the ceiling, anchoring the other end on an old, metal typewriter on his desk. He had cunningly set it to release when the door was opened. The string with its lethal pendant swung toward the doorway right at the level of my forehead -- he either measured exactly to hit me or was very lucky -- and it hit me right between the eyes. I walked in to look around for a minute and the next thing I knew I was knocked out cold.

Nonetheless, I was punished, because I shouldn't have been in my brother's room.

While our transgressions were often similar, Joan had some different punishments for me compared with those received by Mike. Perhaps because he was a boy and was thought physically stronger, the severe punishment usually reserved for Mike was kneeling in the corner, sometimes for hours. He'd stare at the wall and try to be still, but when he shifted his weight, you could hear his bony knees crack against the floor.

"Please, can I get up?" he asked.

"That's another five minutes for asking," Joan would always reply.

My punishment, on the other hand, was being shut in the closet in the front room off the kitchen hallway. Joan would angle a chair against the door to wedge it closed, submerging me in the cool, dark silence. It was certainly quieter and less visible than Mike's tortuous kneeling. Out of sight is out of mind. And perhaps because I was so hidden, I remember being left in the closet for almost three hours.

I have no idea what I did to be placed in there. I had been in trouble with Joan for so many incidents: little things I tried to get away with on purpose, little things I attempted to be more normal at school with my friends, little things she thought I did but didn't, or little slips of the tongue or the hand. The catalyst has long since abandoned my memory, but I can still recall the Saltine crackers she tossed in after me – my impromptu dinner. The crackle of the plastic, the salty taste and the mealy texture.

Only one time do I recall Mike doing something to intervene for me, something really nice for his sister. It was an afternoon when Joan thought we had both mouthed off, which probably meant she told us to do something and we hadn't done it quite quickly enough or to her satisfaction. A subdued groan in disappointment was enough to qualify as mouthing off.

Mike was kneeling in the corner already, and Joan had me by the arm. I made the mistake of not keeping perfectly silent. Something along the lines of, "Oh, Mom" or, "But . . ." escaped my lips, and already tuned to a fever pitch, Joan exploded.

"The mouth on you!" she yelled. Her stride seemed to get longer and louder when she was mad, and her face flushed red, the tendons of her neck standing out. "How many times have I tried to shut that mouth on you?"

In these days of no garbage disposals, the family had a garbage dish in the kitchen, something to throw our organic waste into. One hand pinching my shirt, Joan's other grabbed for the dish and brought it toward me. I could smell the waste on top -- coffee grounds.

Grumbling other assorted angry complaints, Joan got me on my knees and began shoving my head into the dish. I resisted as best I could, tensing up my whole back and neck, but she was standing above me and had leverage. The garbage pressed against my face, which I was trying to keep closed up tight.

After just a few seconds, though, the coffee grounds started to go up my nose and I had to open my mouth to compensate. My whole face was submerged.

Joan's grip was firm and harsh, pressing with what seemed like most her body weight. My eyes opened slightly and burned. The grounds were up in my nose, working their way in my mouth, and I couldn't help but inhale and then cough. Coughing and choking, I struggled for air. I thrashed against her and flailed my arms around, trying to get her hands off of me.

After what felt like a long time, I heard Mike pipe up from where he knelt in the corner. The death grip loosened for a moment and my face emerged from the garbage and I opened my eyes.

Joan's hands were no longer on me. Instead, Mike had grabbed the back of her shirt and was shaking it with all his eleven-year-old might.

"Stop it," he was saying. "Stop it."

Then he caught my eye. His own were wide and scared, as if he wasn't sure about what he was doing.

"Get out of here!" he yelled.

And I admit, I didn't really look back, but just slipped and slid through the spilled garbage out of the back door and into the yard, wiping coffee grounds out of my eyes. I was retching and coughing all the time, heaving in an attempt to catch my breath.

I don't remember what happened to Mike or what passed when I got back to the house that evening. So much about that period is a blur. But I do remember what submersion in those coffee grounds felt and tasted like: bitter and dirty, like being drowned in mud and buried alive at the same time.

*

St. Paul's School was adjacent to St. Paul's Church, and the former was just as brick, dark, foreboding and Catholic as the latter. The classrooms and even the textbooks seemed like they'd been the same for years, maybe decades, and the teachers seemed like the oldest people I could imagine on the planet. Those days were firmly in the era of corporal punishment at school, and the students would often get their knuckles rapped with a ruler. For more serious violations, there was a paddle in the principal's office, though I never got sent there.

Nonetheless, I often did come to school with the marks of my abusive home life on my body. My entire childhood, I remember hurting, being in pain of one type or another. Bruises were common on my upper arms, rear end and knees -- but then again, they were fairly common on the body of any active child. Because of the way Joan beat me, most of the marks left behind could be chalked up by the casual observer to just such juvenile exuberance. Though that may have made things easier for her, I don't think it was planned; she seemed to truly think she was doing the right thing, the only thing, I think.

The hardest to explain to the outside world, however, were the fat lips and black eyes, which resulted mostly from firm slaps across the face. Baseball games, neighborhood bullies, plain clumsiness -- there were natural assumptions for the facial wounds, too. I've found that people -- even teachers -- tend to leap to easy, innocuous explanations first, genuinely hoping they prove to be true. But when a child attends school not once, not twice, but repeatedly with a bruised, swollen face, that's when questions inevitably arise.

Obliquely, I had been asked about these tell-tale signs of abuse before. "What happened?" and "Who did you fight? -- What's the other guy look like?" were common enough questions. Usually, I evaded answering at all. When forced into a corner, I was honest and said that my mother had done it, had made those marks. Children would automatically respond with, "What did you do?" Then they'd brush it off, as kids so often are able to brush off the tragic. Adults, on the other hand -- most of them knew my mother, of course, and how small she was -- rolled their eyes at me in disbelief. If they credited my story at all, it was the attitude of the times to let a family handle itself within itself, to raise their children how they saw fit and wash their own dirty laundry.

I was forced to go to confession once a week and it was something I dreaded, mostly because the one thing that I hated most about my life was the one thing I wasn't supposed to talk about, even in confession. In fact, every time we got home from confession, Joan would make me repeat what I'd said.

"I know you sinned. What did you tell him you did? How many Hail Marys did he give you? How many Our Fathers?"

I listed off the sins I'd related to the priest, genuine sins that I'd committed, even if they were tiny like most children's confessed transgressions. I would say what he prescribed in penance, and without fail, she'd say, "Ha! You thought you'd get away with only that?" Then she'd add punishment of her own to my penance.

One day when I was feeling especially frustrated and hurt, I decided that confession was the one place where I could and should tell the truth. I was waiting in line for the confession booth with my sister Chris. She went in before me, then would wait for me to finish. When I'd taken my seat and closed the door tight -- only lines of light from the chinks around the door making a dim glow -- the priest pulled back that thick, soft black curtain.

"Bless me, Father, for I have sinned," I said, the words common on my tongue.

"Good afternoon, my child," replied the shadowy voice.

I listed off a few of my normal, small sins such as little white lies and the coveting of other people's nice things. Then I took a deep breath and blurted out, "And I hate my mother."

On his side of the curtain, the door flew open and I found myself being dragged out of the booth by my ear. The priest hauled me up to my sister and made her swear to take me home, to make sure that I told my mother exactly what I'd just told him.

*So much for the mercy of God*, I thought.

I remember only a few pointed discussions about the visible signs of my abuse, and of those, the most memorable was Ms. Jefferson.

In addition to being one of my favorite teachers, Ms. Jefferson had to be one of the oldest teachers on the faculty of St. Paul's School. She had the wrinkliest skin I'd ever seen on another human being. Crepe-like folds of it enveloped her eyes, which made it look like her eyes were always winking, twinkling. Wrinkles also surrounded her mouth in soft folds, tracing the paths of many smiles. I thought that if I touched her skin, it would be as soft as fleece.

Of course, it helped that she also had a soft personality; a very sweet teacher who you could tell didn't hate her job teaching all us little devils, like other teachers so obviously did.

One afternoon, she pulled me aside in the hallway as school was getting out. Within a few moments, the hall was relatively clear and we were two of the few people left. We stood to the side of the wide, now empty hallway.

"How are you, Lorijane?" she asked. She folded her hands in front of her, looking both prim and friendly.

"I'm okay," I said. I tugged at my skirt. I had been growing, so it hitched up on me farther than it should.

She tilted her head to one side. "Are you certain, Lorijane?"

I nodded.

"You see, I ask because I see that you're often coming to school looking as if someone hurt you. You have so many kinds of bruises."

At this, she gestured toward the side of my face, which was swollen along the cheek bone. My eyes alternated between looking at the floor and glancing up into her sweet, wrinkly eyes.

"Have you been getting into fights with your brother? With any of the kids in the neighborhood?"

"No."

"Is there a bully who picks on you?"

"No."

"And how is your father?"

"He is well."

She frowned at me a little bit, but in a friendly way, as if she was surprised I didn't know that I could tell her the truth.

"Lorijane, I know that you are coming to school hurt. Therefore, someone must me hurting you."

I looked at my shoes for a moment, linking my hands behind my back. As always when pressed, I wasn't going to lie. I had confirmed that strategy when I tried to tell the priest what had been going on. I looked straight up into her face. It was so kind, and filled with love and understanding. She really wanted to know, so she could help me. After a brief moment, I decided it was safe to divulge my sad secret to this kind woman..

"It's my mother, Ms. Jefferson. My mother hits us."

Her head rocked back in shock, pushing her chin into her neck, and her eyebrows furrowed.

"Your mother?" she shook her head. "Lorijane, don't you make up stories now. I know your mother."

"But it's true," I protested, already sorry I'd told her.

She put her hand on my shoulder and together we turned toward the exit of the school.

"No matter what," she said, "No matter what is going on in the world, one should never speak ill of one's mother."

She said goodbye, trying to maintain her former kind timbre in her voice, and her hand disappeared from my shoulder as I walked out into the street. I continued to walk home as I always did, managing one foot in front of the other.

At first, my eyes filled with tears and the sidewalk in front of me blurred. She was one of my favorite teachers. I loved Ms. Jefferson. And yet . . . she didn't believe me. I told the truth, and she believed I was lying. She must have thought that I was just a wicked little girl like so many others she knew.

She must think I'm a wicked little girl, too, just like the priest thought. Just like Joan thinks I am.

But it was a long walk home. By the time I got back to our salt box colonial on Blackstone Street I had composed myself into the same state of mind I usually had coming home: wary, ready and tense.

In the kitchen I saw baby Michelle in the wooden high chair, where she was elevated and strapped in away from any possible trouble she could get in to. But she was crying. She obviously had been for some time, because her face was as red as a tomato and slick with tears. The moisture was sticking thin strands of baby hair to her cheek in little curls.

She must have been about 18 months old. I was seven or maybe eight. I was gripped with fear as I looked upon the scene, knowing that Joan wouldn't put up with this situation very long, and that she did not discriminate by age when it came to punishing children for sins committed against her.

Joan reached the end of her rope just as I crossed the threshold, yelling, "Stop that damn screaming!"

She shook my baby sister with all of her might and the screams became louder. Her mouth was full open in pain and fear, and the ragged breaths that punctuated her cries frightened me. I thought she couldn't breathe.

I scooted as fast as I could over to that chair. I was snapping off the buckle of her restraint by the time I got out the words, "I got it. I'll get her."

Her chubby arms reached for me and I picked her up, letting her wrap her feet around my waist and her hands around my neck. But she didn't stop screaming right away, I knew she wouldn't. Before Joan could say a word I'd shot out of the room and up the stairs to our bedroom, the girls' bedroom.

When I closed the door behind me I started talking to her soothingly and put her down on the floor. "Shhh," I said. "It's okay. It's all going to be okay now."

I pulled out one of my dolls for her to look at, and she started to calm, hiccupping out the last of her crying. Her face was still bright red, looking tight as a drum. Within five minutes Michelle and I were playing happily on the floor, quiet enough that we couldn't be heard through the floor down to the first level.

Michelle's tears had reminded me of my own unshed tears of the afternoon, of Ms. Jefferson. Without realizing I was making a big decision, I started talking to my little sister, knowing she was too small to understand.

"I know the truth, Michelle. I'll always believe you," I said. "I'll be here and I'll protect you, and I'm going to be your big sister no matter what. Okay?"

She smiled at me and giggled, hugging one of my dolls to her toddler chest.

# Chapter Three

To say that I loved my father is an understatement. Dad was the sun in the sky of my childhood, and the sound of his truck pulling into the driveway would have me on my feet and running to jump into his arms and a big bear hug. He smelled of cigarettes and motor oil, and he made up new nicknames for me every day. They were always strange and goofy, like one of his favorites for me, Oils.

I, on the other hand, always called him by his first Dad. After helping him in the yard and the garage for so many years of my childhood -- as far back as I can remember -- I became his junior assistant. He wasn't around a great deal of the time. His commute to the dairy farm where he was a mechanic took an hour, both going and coming home. He left at 5:30 in the morning most days, stopping at Arnold's coffee shop in town for some coffee on the way, wearing matching blue work pants and a work shirt with a tool belt slung over his shoulder and a name badge on one side of his chest. By the time he returned home, his tan work boots -- which he called his Tyroleans -- were so dirty from walking the dairy farm's mechanical area that Joan wouldn't allow them in the house. He left them in a reserved spot by the front step, the two empty boots by the door signaling, "Dad's home!" Until he took a shower, he always reeked of engine oil, as if he'd been rolling in it all day, which isn't actually that far from the truth.

After his shower or on days off, he reeked of his cologne, Hai Karate, which no one had the guts to tell him stunk worse than the oil. On those days, he'd wear short-sleeved plaid shirts and jeans, except for church, when he cleaned up quite handsome. That's one thing about Dad, is that he was handsome. He took great time with his hair especially, always sporting a perfectly groomed pompadour. He used what I thought of as "magic sticky stuff" so it would never move but stay stiff and slick no matter what.

But in my childhood memories, Dad wasn't "in" the actual house that often. The yard and the garage were officially his realm, where he could do as he wished and reigned supreme. The garage was where he kept his tools and calendars with scantily clad girls and could blast his music, singing along. He loved country music and taught me all the words to "King of the Road" by Roger Miller. He also loved Babs and Patsy, making up funny new lyrics to songs when he couldn't remember the words. He was an excellent whistler in addition to a singer and boasted he could have been the next Bing Crosby. I heartily agreed because I thought he had the looks for it, with his dark, wavy hair and piercing blue eyes.

Mike showed no interest in much that Dad did, so he never really participated in anything going on in the garage or outside. In fact, the two of them were like oil and water, not knowing what the other was made of and overtly suspicious of the other's intensions. They kept apart, or, when together, kept silent. Therefore, out in the yard and in the garage I was Dad's lone assistant in his domain, and that made me a citizen of that special kingdom, too. I valued all the time we spent together out there, out of the house.

Only I knew where to find some things for Dad while he worked. He was the type to disassemble cars and motors and let the unneeded parts fall where they may. Hubcaps rolled into the tall grasses. Bumpers became rusty. Nuts and bolts were scattered like seeds, as if one day during a spring rain they would sprout whole cars.

Maybe they did, because we certainly had a lot of vehicles of all sorts taking up space in our little auto yard, too, mostly around the perimeter. Sometimes we owned them, the product of some trade or deal that Dad made. Others were owned by people who couldn't or didn't want to fix them, who never came back for them.

I loved it when Dad sent me on errands to try to find certain parts.

He'd ask, "Can you find me a 1964 Impala side mirror?" And I'd scoot off into the tall grasses, dappled with pools of sun and shadow from the leafy trees above. I knew the layout of the land better than anyone. I was like the librarian of auto parts, and I found that mirror for him. It didn't need to be the same color or anything and it might have a little crack, but give Dad some screws and some Bondo putty, and he could make it work, make it drivable.

When I was younger, unable to help a great deal, I remember hanging around while Dad repaired a few of the town's school buses. I think it was all the town's school buses, one by one. There was once a church van, as well.

Dad was the unofficial and informal car repair shop of Blackstone, and he was also informal about payment. If a customer -- in that small town, every customer was more like a friend -- didn't have the money to pay for their repairs, he was known to take whatever you could give in trade. He'd traded for a go-kart that he fixed up for the kids, and we had a great time tearing around the neighborhood in that small, metal projectile of looming death. One time we got chickens and the fresh eggs they laid. Another time a customer provided us with venison enough to eat for a full year, and in retrospect I wonder how he continued to keep fresh meat coming year-round. Once, Dad even came home leading a horse. I have no idea what we eventually did with the horse, but the memory of the beast standing in our back yard is vivid.

As I got older, I was given more work to do and I loved every minute of it. Every child wants to feel special and useful, and around Dad, that meant getting to know cars.

One thing I did was detail the cars, thoroughly clean them inside and out until they looked their absolute best. I was a meticulous child, and so I did a meticulous job. I brushed out the car's carpet and interior with a little straw broom, there being no vacuums for such jobs back then. I oiled the leather seats until they shone -- after I'd searched them in and out for lost change, my kid-sized hands finding every lost coin. I'd use a scrub brush to wipe the dirt of many miles from the white-wall tires, using a special solution of Dad’s to fill little cracks and make the tires shine as if they were wet.

I was fascinated to find that one car had its trunk in the front and its engine in the back, a Chevy Corvair. Other times, I got to clean out really old cars from the '30s and '40s. I specifically remember one impressive black antique car, sleek and smart like in the movies, if quite a bit more rundown. It had a posing woman for a hood ornament. Dad called it "the gangster-mobile," and because it didn't run well, we had it for a while. My friends from the neighborhood and I would play cops and robbers in it, always pretending we were making a fast getaway.

The detailing was fun. I think I would have done it even if the customers didn't pay me. The bit of spending money I earned was just icing on the cake.

The same goes for Dad’s work, which he did on the side of his job at the dairy. When his paycheck came from the dairy, he had to hand it over whole to Joan. But when he made some money hand-to-hand from a customer for fixing a car, that was his -- or at least he was better able to hide it from Joan. He had a hidden jar in the garage where he would keep those bonus dollars, which were his fun money, his cigarette and whatever money.

As I got older, I was allowed to help with more complicated parts of Dad's repair work. I'd sit on the concrete drive outside his garage and hand him tools when he was under a car, only his legs sticking out, or when he was waist deep under the hood. I knew all of his tools, including the English and metric measurements for all the wrenches, although metric was a new phenomenon then. I could hold things in place while he screwed them together. I could sit in the driver's seat and start the car, over and over, so he could see and hear if the problem had been solved.

When there were papers to read, I could do that for him, Dad being "not so good" at that. When there was complicated math during a deal, he'd often ask, "Now how much does that make, Lorijane?" I'd add it up or subtract it for him. When he was hot in the summer, I was sent to the house for his iced coffee: a large iced tea glass with seven ice cubes -- exactly seven -- filled with coffee and milk. I loved the smell of it as I carefully carried the refreshing beverage to him, but I never did develop a taste for the cold coffee treat.

When there wasn't bargaining or singing going on, Dad would talk to me. Although, perhaps he wasn't directing the talk at me but just out into the world at large. He'd let out a constant stream of talk, about anything in the world. He'd tell stories about his days in the Navy and how Navy boys were always up to no good, backing up that assertion with evidence of all the trouble he got into. He'd talk about his friends, our family and even the car deals and trades he made, how he'd gotten the better end of the bargain. He'd call all his talking "the skinny," meaning that he would give me the skinny -- the real, straight talk -- about anything.

My extra pair of hands were vital when Dad needed to use his homemade winch to lift transmissions or whole engines out of the hood cavity of the cars he was working on. The chain fall as he called it was a basic, sturdy chain slung four 2-by-4 pieces of wood bolted together and bolted into the thickest part of the old tree, which grew right next to the concrete drive in front of his garage. You yanked on the chain and the transmission you needed out rose up into the air. Once the part was elevated, the makeshift brake to keep it there was a big Sears and Roebuck screwdriver, wedged between the links of the chain to hold it in place. It worked quite well, like so many things Dad hacked together with his own two hands.

When he took out the transmissions of cars, it was my job, to balance it aloft and keep it from spinning until he did whatever he needed to do. Then we'd lower it back into place, the chain fall still holding its weight as Dad refastened all the various parts to the transmission.

I wore my sneakers and a pair of bib shorts, overalls Dad had cut the legs off of for them to be more comfortable in summer. I was about eight or nine and I was straddling the fender and guiding the chain as Dad fixed the transmission of a Ford Fairlane. He was on a rolling dolly underneath the car. I could see snippets of his face and his work clothes through the various engine parts as he moved around. I sometimes handed him a tool, or nudged a tool closer to his hand with my foot so he could reach it.

He'd said that something was stuck, that he'd have to go under, so I needed to man the screwdriver serving as the pin that held everything together.

"Don't let it drop now, because I'm going to be right under," he said.

I dreaded the times when he said that, when I could see him like that beneath me. It was only me that was standing between him and a major accident, a serious accident that would hurt my favorite person in the world. He trusted me. I didn't know if I trusted me, though. I was only in the second or third grade, and taking someone's life into your hands was frightening.

That Ford Fairlane just wasn't a lucky car. That afternoon wasn't a lucky day. I was straddling the fender, holding the screwdriver with both hands, and I saw the metal shaft begin to bend. It was surreal, like those people bending spoons with the power of their minds.

"Um, Dad," I said, my voice quavering.

"Huh?"

The bend in the screwdriver got more severe and I panicked, yelling, "Dad! Dad! It's breaking! Dad!"

It was my worst fears coming true. The bend broke. Both of my hands were flung away from where I'd been holding the screwdriver, now holding air. The transmission dropped and the chain followed suit, rattling wildly as it plummeted back to earth.

"Dad!" I screamed, my last vision seeing his chest beneath the heavy machinery.

I tried to spring off the fender to help him, to go to where he was and pull him out. But the moment my leg hit the pavement, I fell. Something had just given out when I tried to use my leg. I was lying stomach down on the ground, my elbows and palms skinned raw, when Dad appeared from around the side of the car. Somehow, he'd known that I was warning him and rolled out from underneath the impending megalith just in time. Perhaps he was just lucky. There he was, walking, though, and I took a deep breath of relief.

"Are you okay?" he asked, looking me over as if I'd been hurt. It fell, and . . . are you okay?"

I noticed he'd scraped his head on something and was bleeding a little, but he looked basically whole, all his parts still attached. I was greatly relieved. Dad studied me for a moment, as if wondering why I was on the ground. Then he started running toward me.

"Oh my god," he gasped. "Are you okay? What's wrong? What happened?"

"I don't know. The screwdriver broke and -- "

"You're bleeding!"

Sure enough, I looked down to see that there was a puddle of blood growing under my thigh. I turned over to take a look and the wound became visible. It was a puncture; the metal shaft of the screwdriver had hit my leg with the force of a bullet, traveled clean through and out the other side and then lodged in the tree. It was bad. I could see the blood leaking out slowly I was scared.

Dad said, "Good god, what happened," but it wasn't a question. He was already taking off his shirt, which he then wrapped around my leg. He knotted the edges, pulling it uncomfortably tight. Like a damsel in distress, he scooped me into his arms and ran toward the nearest form of transportation, which happened to be his car. I sat on the front bench, built for two, as he took the driver's seat, and we made it to the hospital as fast as we could.

I needed a tetanus shot and a few stitches and I couldn't walk normally for a while, but I had really cool scars; one on the front of my thigh where it flew in, and one on the side of my knee where it exited. Dad found the rest of the screwdriver shaft embedded in the tree later.

Thc incident had scared me greatly, but in the end I wore the scars with pride. Number one . . . I'd been brave and helpful. And number two . . . my Dad had rushed to my rescue, and I felt loved and protected, something I rarely felt in my family.

I was obviously a child to think that way, because it's true that I often got into my worst scrapes when I was around Dad. For instance, one of the best treats we could get was a truck ride in Dad's car to Lowell's Dairy for ice cream, which was two towns over. It was a different time back then, and we weren't even wearing seat belts. Instead, I'd kneel on the bench seat of his truck and play with his CB radio. It was a running game to try to find someone farther and farther away. From Massachusetts, we'd gotten as far as Kentucky. My handle was Spider Legs, one of Dad's nicknames for me, because I was both skinny and tall as I grew toward adolescence.

At one point in the journey for ice cream, we had to take Dead Man's Curve. I think every town has a Dead Man's Curve somewhere nearby, a sharp and scary stretch of road where accidents were known -- or at least rumored -- to occur. I loved Dead Man's Curve.

"Go faster! Go faster!" I'd say to Dad as we approached the bend.

He raised his eyebrows, pretending to consider it, then complied as he always did. His beat up, old truck would accelerate. It was a blue Ford of indeterminate year. Various years, in fact, because the parts of so many trucks had been cobbled into it over the stages of its long life. Parts of it must have been held together with nothing but Bondo. It rattled and moaned, which actually made the scary atmosphere of speeding on Dead Man's Curve all the better.

It was normally fine, the thrill dissolving back into the anticipation of ice cream. Then one time, the truck's tire veered just slightly off the road, bouncing onto the dirt shoulder. Because of the speed we were going, that little bounce was enough to make the truck rock up and down once, hard, knocking my teeth together, and knocking open the passenger door, from which I spilled out into the world beyond the moving car. I rolled down the hill tumbling along on my sides, my hands over my face, and landed 10 feet from the road in prickly bush, one that leaves the sharp prickles stuck all over your body and clothes.

I saw the brake lights flash hard and heard the tires squeal to a halt. Within seconds there was Dad, asking if I was okay, looking over my arms and legs for signs of serious harm. But other than a few cuts and bruises, I was completely whole and essentially unscathed.

"I fell in the prickles," I offered.

"That you did," he said. “Don’t tell your mother!”

I giggled, high on the pumping adrenaline. He was worried and sheepish, mortified that he'd sped up in the first place and that his truck had so betrayed him. I was a mess of prickles and we headed home, where he had to shower me off with a garden hose to get all of them off before I went inside and to bed with the stern warning of “Don’t tell your mother!”

I think I enjoyed evenings with Dad the most, when he finally took off his boots and came inside. After dinner, we'd go into the family room to relax, a room decked out with brown plaid furniture, our console TV and a wood-burning fireplace surrounded with built-in bookshelves, which housed all the Encyclopedia Britannicas. I'd sit in on the arm of the chair and we would read the newspaper, because he enjoyed knowing what was going on in the world. "What do you want first? The front page? Sports? Dear Abby? Want to hear who is selling their house?" I'd ask him.

He'd pick his choice and we'd make our way through most of the paper until "All in the Family" came on the television. Then I'd lie belly down on the floor and watch, too. Dad loved Archie Bunker.

"Now there's a man after my own spirit," he would say.

*

I idolized Dad. There was no doubting that. My entire heart belonged to him. However, even Dad had his flaws, I knew.

He made it my job to pick up his cigarette butts, for instance. He was a very heavy smoker and, much like his discarded parts and cars, he'd just toss them anywhere. Outside they littered the ground. Ever the inventor, he made me a tool for the purpose: a long stick or broom handle with a nail on the end, so I could stab each one without bending down. But he could have just not thrown them anywhere and everywhere in the first place, I thought.

Other times Dad would come home from an evening of hanging out and drinking with his friends in town. The one friend of his in particular I remember was Bob Schram, whom Joan didn't like. He had a reputation for being shady and was known as Schram the Scam.

Bob's wife was nicknamed Lacquer by my dad. She had black hair in an up do that was so shiny and dark he swore she lacquered it at night. She wore dresses and black cat eye styled glasses. She smoked heavily and always came to the door with a cigarette in hand. Their son David was one of Mike's friends. They were an odd family.

Now Dad wasn't an alcoholic by any means, but he loved an occasional party. There were times when he woke me up with his off-key singing outside in the front yard, where he was having trouble making it up the three cement steps. Into the music, he'd bang out the percussion on the siding of the house. It was usually me who went down and helped him take his boots off, and push him toward the couch.

And he wasn't always the sharpest tool in the shed. He seemed a caring man -- he'd stop his truck to let turtles cross the road -- but he wasn't always very smart. When I complained about the tapping of one of our trees against my bedroom window at night, he set up a ladder and brought up his saw. He made a clean cut through the offending branch, but the ladder happened to be leaning against the now sawn off end of that branch, and he tumbled down with it.

First and foremost of his flaws -- of the things I didn't understand about Dad -- was his reaction to Joan's extreme violence with us kids. If he happened to be nearby when Joan started to get worked up, yelling and stomping, he'd come into the room and stop it. Many a time I saw him grab her hand in mid air, his muscles visibly working to restrain her.

"Joan," he'd say firmly. "Knock it off."

After a moment, she took a breath and calmed down. She was still steaming over whatever had upset her, of course, but the lid was on the kettle, for a time.

Then he'd pick up whatever kid had been hurt and put us back on our feet. Kneeling down to dust off our pants or wipe our face, he'd say, "It's going to be fine."

He had never hit Joan, and never raised a hand except to restrain hers. But he had also never intervened in how she beat us kids unless he was there at the moment, unless he happened to walk in while the scene was unfolding. Plus, if he were in the house at all, Joan kept her distance and her temper the best she could.

But the problem with that was that he was often away, gone most of the day to work or into the refuge of his garage. The majority of the time he was only there for the aftermath, when his voice would growl low and mean, "Joan, have you been hitting those kids? It's too much. No more."

But there would always be more. I often told him about some of the things she did to me and Michelle and Mike, talking about it in detail in the garage or as we rode in his truck. I showed him my bruises. He made vague promises about making things better or that things were going to change, but nothing ever did.

It was like he was one of the many turtles that populated the semi-wild land around our neighborhood: he was able to pull his head out of the world and into the dark whenever he was overwhelmed. With her education and her violent temper, Joan overwhelmed him. It was easier for him to pretend the situation wasn't that bad, that everything was in control. It was perhaps unconscious, but was willful ignorance nonetheless.

But I loved him. With him I felt more loved and protected than with anyone else in the world.

I knew that Joan didn't love him. She called him a horse's ass or a worthless son-of-a bitch. She said he wasn't right, that he was dishonest and often accused him of lying and keeping part of his paycheck that she needed to run the household.

I never saw them kiss or hug, or even hold hands. Whenever he came into the house, she'd yell for him to take off his muddy boots and then tell him, "You stink. You smell like a cigarette." They called each other Joan and Frank, never any other endearing or pet name.

"Do you see this?" she'd yell at him. "Do you see the chaos that is our lives? This is all your fault with your ignorant, low-class, lazy attitude."

Later he would come to me and whisper, "What did that word mean? What did she say?" He had far too much pride to ask her himself.

They did share a bedroom, but more often than not -- especially as I got older -- Joan took to sleeping on the couch in the living room. She said that Dad snored, and I knew that to be true so didn't think much of it.

When we kids got in trouble, sometimes she would grab each one of us by the shirtfront in turn and menacingly repeat one of her favorite sayings: "I didn't want any of you. I hate all of you," she said. Then she would tell us horrible, hateful things about Dad, accusing him of vile acts.

I'd keep my mouth shut in front of Joan, but I knew they weren't true. Though I couldn't have expressed the idea at the time, I knew that there was no way to tell the difference between a truth or a lie under this roof. Everything was mixed up and manipulated and mean. My brain worked in a kind of protection mode at all times. We lived in a war zone, and evil forces were pervasive in every corner of the house. I had to stay on my toes at all times.

For my own part, I knew not to lie, or at least not to be caught in one. The consequence for that kind of transgression was lava soap in the mouth. But I knew that Joan was a consummate liar. Later in the quiet times upstairs, I'd tell Michelle, "That ain't true, Michelle. None of what Mom says about him is true."

# Chapter Four

It was summer, a lovely summer afternoon, and I was sitting on the front steps of our house watching cars drive by. The sun was warm on my legs and the sky was blue, and like most kids, I loved staring into the depth of the sky, amazed at how big the world really was and how small all we people really were. I looked for shapes in the clouds.

From the front room I could hear the radio and Joan singing along with the music. She was ironing, a hot task on a hot day, and so the windows were open to capture what breeze they could. There was the hissing noise of the iron's steam as she worked, tapping her foot to the beat of the music.

She was obviously in her own little world as she pressed the clothes and linens. There were no distractions. Baby Michelle was asleep in her crib in the next room and I was out of sight through the screen door, and I think for that brief moment, she thought she was alone. Not a mother or a wife, not responsible for anything but the task in front of her, and happily humming and tapping her toes.

And then Michelle woke up. It was a normal kind of waking up from her nap, about the same time and the same way she usually woke, with a little groan and a stretch. A little whimpering cry as she came to and tried to figure out where she was.

The ironing stopped, and I turned my head to look through the screen door. Joan had frozen, her shoulders tensed up to her ears. And then I heard what I called "the stomp," the changing of her tiny little footsteps into the powerful, booming stomps of her anger.

She stomped the few paces over to the screen door and shouted, "You woke the baby!"

I looked back at her in puzzlement and shock. Sitting there as silently as I had been, the assertion was ludicrous, but I dared not argue with her. Her face was red, her neck tendons standing out, and I knew that face. It was the face of unreasonable rage, the stage of her anger in which it didn't matter what had happened, what was right or wrong. She was right and I was wrong, so step out of the path of the speeding train.

I just glanced down from her glare to the ground and said nothing.

But then she turned, and I heard the stomp headed toward the corner room where Michelle was still fussing.

She was going to hurt the baby.

The thought clicked in my head and within three stomps, I had swung open the screen door and barreled into the room, squeezing by Joan's right side with arms outstretched toward the baby, trying to reach her first. By a hair's breadth, my fingers skimmed Michelle's shirt, grabbed on and slid her against my chest, hugging her near.

"Lorijane!" Joan growled. She reached for the collar of my sleeveless shirt, but I was just out of reach. Her fingertips brushed the back of my neck but found no purchase.

"You're not going to touch her," I said, not loud but firmly.

"Lorijane." The word was a warning, drawn out and rumbling. Her hands were in fists by her side and her eyes were blazing. Rage was like a drug in her bloodstream. Once the anger was incited, it was an unstoppable fever that had to run its course.

And I knew that hurting that 18-month-old baby was not beyond her when she was this worked up -- worked up from out of the blue, from nothing, because of nothing. Even if her hand was larger than all of Michelle's chubby, little face, that hadn't stopped her from deliberately hurting Michelle with all the might of her stringy frame. I had seen it before, her picking up Michelle by one arm and her little shoulder socket strained by her own weight . . . and I couldn't let that happen again.

I ducked past Joan and dodged back toward the front door, scampering across the lawn as fast as I could and through the line of trees into the neighbor's yard. I heard my mother yelling behind me, hurling insults at me, calling me an ungrateful brat and worse. As I ran, I saw the face of our neighbor, Mrs. Davidson, through her window. Our eyes met briefly and she looked at me so sadly. Her head shook just slightly, then she looked down. I continued running.

At least that day, no one got hit.

It was a strategy I was finding to be very effective in keeping Michelle and myself safe from Joan, ever since I'd made a pact with myself that I would be her protector, her defender.

Agreed, Michelle was a fussy baby at times, and even those with nerves of steel would be tried in keeping patient, but she was kind of a chubby little kid with very unkept hair and I didn't want her to go through what my brother and I had. I'd take a bath with her, singing her little songs while she splashed in the tub. I wiped off the dirt and grime from her knees after she played outside as well as the food from her face after she ate. I changed her diapers and helped dress her in the mornings. And every afternoon when I got home from school I'd creep up to her crib and gently wake her to whisk her away somewhere to play.

The games we played were designed to keep her safe, too. We played the quiet game, not speaking, using only hand gestures. We tiptoed around the upstairs level, and whoever made the floor creak would lose. And we played hide-and-go-seek. Sometimes I would be "it" and try to find her. Other times we would hide together so I could show Michelle all my favorite places to disappear from sight. We'd cuddle up close in the bathroom cabinet or under the bed and just be together, silently. There was a crawlspace adjacent to my bedroom which became a secret little fort, where we kept certain toys and dolls, where we withdrew from the world, hidden away from the cruelties of Joan. Sometimes Michelle would fall asleep with her head on my lap or on my shoulder, her sweet baby breath on my skin.

At dinner, Michelle sat in the old, wooden high chair, the same one that had once held me -- and likely my older sisters Hope and Chris. I usually sat in the chair nearest to her so I could help feed her. She was still eating pureed baby food at this point, and though she could hold on to a spoon, she usually needed help to get some of the food in her mouth rather than on her face or shirtfront.

I had done something wrong this one night that I remember, a vivid memory alive with danger, even after decades. Joan was yelling at me for one reason or another, and she was raging mad, breathing hard through her nostrils like a bull. And suddenly -- my hand, holding the baby's spoon, was poised in mid air, frozen -- Joan's arm reached out and swept clear the tray of the high chair, right in front of Michelle, where there had been two jars of baby food.

The food flew like a pitched baseball and exploded on the floor. Joan's quick movement and the noise of the shattering glass startled Michelle, who began to cry tears of fear and confusion. I sat there with my jaw hanging open, unsure what had just happened or how to react.

Hands on her hips, surveying the mess and still breathing hard, Joan said, "Well, you better clean that up then." It was a control game. She needed me to do what she said, to reinforce her authority.

I looked over at Mike. His face was turned down, intent on his plate, but he met my eyes momentarily. The look clearly said, "Don't ask me. You're on your own, sister."

I closed my jaw. "Okay," I said. "Hold on."

Michelle's wailing was loud in my ears and she was reaching for me from her high chair, her fingers opening and closing on thin air. I wanted to just calm her down for a moment before I bent down to the task.

"I told you to clean that up," Joan repeated.

"Okay, just one second," I said as politely as possible, indicating that I would accomplish both tasks within just a few seconds.

"Clean up your mess when I tell you to clean up your mess," said Joan from above me, her teeth clenched. "Don't you talk back to me."

I was silent as I attempted to remain calm, for the baby's sake. Joan shoved my head toward the floor, then released my hair. My right hand flew to the back of my head, and I was surprised and relieved to find that my hair was still attached, though it flared pain like a rug burn.

Michelle was wailing even louder now, kicking her feet in the chair. I saw Joan moving toward her, her veins still bulging in anger. I jumped to my feet and beat her to the baby, sliding her out of the chair as if she had been greased. I had luckily forgotten to latch the safety belt around her waist, which bought me the split second of time I needed to overtake Joan and rescue Michelle from the imminent assault.

And for the first time ever, I pushed her. I screamed, "No!" and I pushed my mother out of the way, hard enough to make her stumble against the wall, hitting her shoulder. Her eyes met mine and glowered as if they were on fire. She was so enraged and bright red with anger that I wouldn't have been surprised if she had been hot to the touch. I didn't want to wait around to find out.

With Michelle's legs wrapped tightly around my waist I ran up the stairs and into my room, slamming the door. I skidded to my knees near the thigh-high door to the crawlspace that sat beside my room. I moved the panel out of the way and shoved in little Michelle feet first, and she landed on her diaper-padded bottom. Then I dropped to my stomach and started to army crawl my way in behind her. Only my knees and feet were still in my bedroom, when I heard the door open and Joan come in.

"Lorijane!" she yelled. "You get back here! Now!"

Her fingers reached for my ankles, but I was able to slip them in just in time, slamming the panel back in place behind me. I started piling whatever I could from the crawlspace against the door; heavy boxes, discarded furniture, anything. And all the while she was yelling, calling my name, banging on the door with her fists. I thought her hand was going to bust all the way through the drywall to the other side, reaching for us like a claw through a cage.

But we were silent. All I had to do was look at Michelle and put one finger to my lips, and she knew what to do. She nodded and hiccupped the last of her tears. I sat cross-legged and she crawled into my lap. And we sat companionably in the dark, rocking just slightly, like people in a tornado shelter waiting out the storm and hoping for the best.

Joan slowly lost momentum and volume. Banging and pushing on the door, banging and pushing, then pausing to yell out more threats. Finally, there was silence and I let there be silence for a very long time before we moved all the boxes out of the way and re-emerged.

We crept to our beds and went to sleep with the house quiet around us, hoping there wouldn't be too much hell to pay in the morning.

*

Michelle was still so small, still not in school, still the baby of the family in so many ways. Mike and I, on the other hand, were inevitably growing like weeds, sprouting oversized feet and hands as well as often sporting clothes that began to reveal an extra slice of wrist or ankle.

We were also growing attitudes. So dissimilar in almost every way -- he was explosive and often cruel, while I tried to be dependable and caring -- we nonetheless had an uneasy alliance when it came to dealing with Joan. We may have hated one another, actively hated one another, but a team of two was better than one when faced with a common enemy.

Mike was around 12 or 13, and he was as tall as -- if not taller than -- tiny, little Joan. I was 10 or 11 and was edging up to her chin, a few inches from being able to look her straight in the eye.

We were inured to the violence, thought it was inevitable no matter what we did, so we took little liberties. We rolled our eyes. We pulled faces. We imitated Joan's voice telling us to do something. We hid all of these from her, and disguised sarcasm in even the most dutiful of responses, so that even "Yes, Mom" sounded like talking back to the attuned ear.

In other words, we were absolutely normal kids of that age, but Joan didn't handle normal very well. She'd already raised two kids to adulthood, so she'd been through it before, and it was obvious that her nerves and her will were frayed, strained to the point of breaking. The violence and anger were even closer to the surface than in the past.

But after years of experience, now we were prepared.

When she burst into a rage, Mike and I would take off in opposite directions, using hand gestures to agree who went which way. She couldn't chase both of us, so only one got a punishment. The next time around, we switched routes to take turns with the beatings. Around the house, I could still use the crawl space next to my room. But we also knew how to run into the living room and dive behind the couch, leaving no trailing shoes or clothes for her to grab. Skinny and stringy, both Mike or I could fold ourselves behind that sofa in a way that she couldn't reach us, even kneeling on the floor, her whole arm stretching. She was forced to move the entire couch to get to the offender, and by the time she'd move one end, Mike or I would be up, out faster than a wild rabbit.

We had all sorts of schemes and mechanisms -- coping mechanisms -- to handle Joan, which is really the only way a child can thwart an adult. Adults are ultimately stronger and more powerful. By the time the chase was over and Joan had finally caught me, she would be twice as angry than when the incident started, and I'd get twice the beating. Even if I avoided half of the beatings I would have gotten, I suffered twice as much, making the whole bargain rather even and futile. But protecting myself and my baby sister were the only rebellion I had.

Every once in a while, the police were called in to handle "domestic incidents" at our house. I knew some of the officers by name because they were kind, if brusque, and their last names were printed on the chest of their uniforms. As far as I know it was usually Mrs. Davidson, our next door neighbor, who called them in. It was across her lawn that I often fled, always followed by Joan yelling, "Get back here, now!" or "Yeah, you better run, you brats. I'm going to send you off to the foster home!"

The police would drive up in their impressive car with the lights on top and troop up to the front door. They'd talk to Joan for a few minutes and deliver a little lecture. She'd nod her head in the right places, adding something about "The kids these days . . . they don't listen, they act up!" Then the cops would tip their hats to Joan and drive away. Abuse was handled so much differently in those days, as more of a minor disturbance than a crime.

Joan had subtle ways of torturing me too that didn't leave marks. She would do the laundry out of the hallway laundry basket on Saturdays. If my underwear were inside out I would get hit. If my underwear was a little wet I owed her a quarter. My underwear was often a little wet. Not wet through and through, and never messy. A little wet because it hurt so bad to urinate that I would often hold it in for hours and hours. I remember out on the hardtop at St. Paul's playground I would kneel to play jacks and secure the heel of one of my feet into my crotch to prevent the urge to urinate. Why? I have no idea. This went on for at least two years and all I remember is being very irritated down there and the urine burned. The soiling was never more than a few drops but it was enough to infuriate Joan nonetheless.

Much of those years is rather patchy in my memory. Some events are crystal clear and others are completely absent, creating huge, black gaps of space in the story of my life. I can only imagine why my mind chooses to block it out. Certainly, memory loss and confusion are effects of child abuse, and I know that played a large part. But although memory cannot back me up, a lot of that loss surrounds memories of Mike. There are feelings of dread hovering around the figure of my bizarre, angry and mean big brother that I cannot explain and likely will never be able to.

But there is one that stands out in bold relief, one memory of Mike that I will never be able to forget, marking a turning point of my family's life, going from bad to worse.

We were sitting at the kitchen table early one evening waiting to start dinner. Joan was really a terrible cook -- no one really craved the dinner because of its taste -- and sitting around waiting has a way of making anyone anxious.

I had invited my friend Peggy home for dinner at my house that night. It was a rare occurrence. Ever since I could remember, I always played at other kids' houses and they rarely came to mine. In our neighborhood, most of the moms stayed at home while the dads worked outside the house. Therefore, they seemed aware of Joan's reputation and always gently suggested that we kids play in their family's yard, not ours.

As I grew up, I continued to keep friends away on purpose. I never knew what the atmosphere of the house was going to be like and feared being backhanded in front of any friend I decided to bring home. I had been to Peggy's house several times and had discovered it was nothing like my own. When she spoke loudly, I said, "Shhh. What if your mother hears?"

She shrugged and said, "Nothing." There were cookies free for the taking in the kitchen, and smiles and hugs and compliments were freely given and received.

It was the first time I realized that not every family lived the way we did, in constant fear and pain. That unhappiness, in fact, was not a natural and necessary result of coming home. Some people, some families, were happy together. The concept was both a hopeful and fearful one: I hoped that one day I could experience that happiness, and I feared that my friends might find out that my family wasn't like theirs. My family was somehow wrong, rotten and flawed.

That Peggy was there for dinner that night, that night of all nights is something I would regret for years.

The two of us were sitting on one side of the table, across from Mike and Michelle, the latter now big enough to sit in a regular chair and feed herself at meals. Her hair was coming in thicker now, but still held that baby curl around her face. Mike's face was set in the lines of a sneer, as usual, and his hair was trimmed in what we called a brush cut -- military inspired, close cropped to the scalp, almost nonexistent. Joan was the only one standing, moving between the counter and table to finalize the dinner preparation.

Joan was nagging Mike to do something. Take out the trash? Do lawn work? Stop getting in trouble in school? It hardly matters. It could have been any of the above.

The point was that he sassed, as he was growing more and more fond of doing. "What is she going to do?" he would ask me in private. He'd puff up his skinny chest and say, "I'm taller than she is, aren't I?"

At the table that night, the first time she asked him to do something that he'd forgotten, he said, "All right," but the remark dripped with sarcasm.

Joan returned, "I mean it. I'm sick and tired of your sarcastic mouth." You're not worth the effort, any of you. This time you had just better listen up."

With a malicious glint in his eye, Mike said, "Make me."

And so she did.

In one smooth movement, Joan grabbed a black, cast iron skillet from the counter top and stretched out full length, her arm swung toward Mike hitting him square in the back of the head with a clang similar to a sound effect on a Saturday morning cartoon. It must have happened fast, but it seemed like slow motion to me. I tried to yell, "No," but before I could finish that one syllable, Mike had dropped to the kitchen floor like a sack of potatoes.

All the kids threw their chairs back from the table with a squeak and stood up, leaning over and around the table to see what had happened. Mike was face first on the floor, only the back of his head visible -- but the back of his head was where the damage was.

There was a crack, a real fissure, a few inches long. The skin all the way around was red from the blow, but the edges of the cut were purple, then a layer of dusty white. It was bone, or worse. I was looking at my brother's bones, his skull -- with the awful feeling that there may have been some other material mixed in the wound.

"Oh my eeeeww!" I screeched, my shoulders rising up to my chin in disgust.

I saw Joan turn toward me at the noise and raised the skillet in my direction, threatening me for my noise. But I cowered a little and lowered my face. She forgot me and went back to Mike.

He was down for the count a few moments, long enough for us kids to move closer and get a pretty good look at his wound. At first it didn't bleed but remained spookily dry, as if the damage was fake. Looking closer at the bone, I could see other tissue: greyish, puffy, sponge-like.

I thought I could see Mike's brain! As unbelievable as that seems to me today.

At that point the wound began to drip blood very slowly, as if the blood itself had just recovered from the shock and remembered what it was supposed to do. Mike also began to move and come back to his limited senses. He got his hands underneath him, then his elbows, and lifted himself to one knee.

He looked mad. And he was looking right at Joan.

"What did you -- "

His question was cut off by another swing of the iron skillet, this time hitting the side of his head, square on the ear. It was not quite as hard as the first -- Joan hadn't the room to get enough momentum for that -- but the blow still flung him to the side, forcing him back down on an elbow.

He sprang to his feet, anger perhaps kicking in his adrenaline sufficiently to allow him to move so fast. Lord knows, he must have hurt. One hand to his head, the other clenched in a fist at his side, he took a step toward Joan. He leaned forward to show her that he was bigger than her and possibly stronger. She raised the frying pan slightly in response.

No words were exchanged. The silence stretched a few tense seconds. Then Mike clenched his jaw, turned on his heel and left the house. He would stay at friends', and didn't spend much time with the family again.

There are so many things I didn't know and couldn't ask about the incident. I don't know if Peggy told her parents what happened, or if so, how she framed it, or if they were alarmed by the report. Her parents continued to be nice to me when I came over, perhaps overly nice. Did Mike get medical attention? I didn't see how he could have gone without it. What did the doctor say, what did they think? How many stitches did he get? Why didn't the police come and take Joan away in handcuffs?

As a child, I think that my view of the incident might have been both slightly overblown in my own mind and an under-reaction. Could I have perhaps overstated things in my re-telling it at the time? Kids love the gross and grotesque, and I admit that the gross-out factor of seeing what appeared to be brain tissue was certainly scary, but also just a little bit cool, kind of an accomplishment. Perhaps I embellished the gore in my head. I was small at the time, therefore the wound probably appeared very large to me. I often wonder how my adult eyes would see it, if it would appear smaller, but I'll never know. The childhood vision is just too strong. Surely, it was a large, gaping wound. Certainly, I saw things in the injury that no child should be exposed to. Was there exposed muscle?

Probably. Was there bare bone? Possibly. Was there brain tissue? Unlikely, I know -- yet that was what my young eyes thought they saw.

The under reaction part lies in how things just went on, kept on going as if everything was normal. I didn't freak out or break down. I didn't sob into my pillow. I didn’t run away. I didn’t even tell anyone -- the police, the priest, the teachers. We just continued on, minus Mike.

I talked to my sister Hope about it later when she came over. It was chaos at the house and she’d only heard part of the story.

"He just went down like this," I told her, making hand gestures. Pointing to my own head, I added, "And it hit him right here, with the edge. Oh, it was so gross. You could see pink and white and grey, and it was kind of oozing."

"Lorijane," she said, in a tone that urged me to slow down, to take it easy. "Come on, now."

"No, it was really gross," I insisted. "It was his skull! We could see his skull!"

She shook her head. She didn't think I was lying, but she knew well enough that I would tell the story to make it as grotesque and impressive as possible. True enough, but I knew what I saw. I told her that Mike had left, that I didn't think he was coming back.

"They've had it out before," Hope said. "He'll be back."

A few days later Mike did return for a bag of his clothes, but that was it. He began to live with his friend Chris a few streets over, full time. We'd see him around the neighborhood now and then, on weekends and in the afternoon, but he wouldn't come to play with us or even have a conversation. He would just meet my eye and nod a little, acknowledging my presence, and then walk on. It wasn't too much later that Mike and his friends were making Molotov cocktails out of junkyard bottles. I often wondered if smoke I smelled was a bonfire set by my estranged brother -- or perhaps a neighborhood cat who had accidentally wandered into his clutches.

When Mike was 17, he disappeared from the area.

We didn't talk about it at home. Uncomfortable as I was around him, I was a little bit glad to see him go, for my sake. I wouldn't have to deal with him or his 'tickling" or his torture. I was simultaneously happy for him to have gone for his own sake, because I saw the look in Joan's eyes that night. She hungered to end it, and I think had he stayed, she would have killed him that very night. She simply could not live with someone who no longer feared her.

Joan and Dad had five kids, and had seen two of them off already, out of the nest relatively young. Mike being absent was one less mouth to feed and back to clothe, just at the time when -- even as a child I could see -- money was getting tight.

*

It started several years before Mike left, that I noticed money, or the lack thereof, becoming an issue in my life. I was at St. Paul's Catholic School, a very traditional school where all the students wore matching dresses and shirts and ties.

My clothes were hand-me-downs from my sisters' school days long ago, or second hand clothes that Joan bought at the thrift store that were sold cheaper than the new ones. The problem came when I hit a growth spurt, began to sprout overnight and my skirts became tighter and tighter, shorter and shorter.

The kids at school stood in a row for inspection. The fat and thin, the tall and short, all lined up and made essentially identical. A teacher would walk the line, making sure buttons were fastened and ties correctly knotted. Special attention, however, was paid to the hemlines. The teachers even carried a ruler; in case the eye was unsure, they could measure exactly how much skin was being revealed above the knee.

I looked down to mine and inwardly groaned. I could see my knobby knees and at least an inch of skin below my hemline.

"Too short," the teacher said.

"I'm sorry."

"You were warned last week."

"I know, Ma'am."

She looked at me hard, then said, "Very well."

She took the ruler and snapped it against the tender valley at the back of my knees. It was a slap not of viciousness, but simple efficiency.

I went home to tell Joan about my skirt -- again, because she'd known for weeks that I needed a new one. She waved me away.

St. Paul's kept good track of the Catholic families in our area, especially the families that both had children enrolled in the school and attended mass on Sundays regularly. Again, because they were very traditional, they didn't just pass the basket during mass for donations to the church. Instead, they expected a full 10 percent tithe from all the Catholic families in the parish. Because the Catholic religion seems to thrive on guilt, there was a chalkboard outside the old brick church that listed the names of families who were in arrears with their tithes. I assume they thought the board a "gentle reminder," but everyone knew it was in fact the wall of shame.

One Sunday, our family's name appeared on the wall of shame. We noticed it as we walked up the front steps, and I think I saw the biggest reaction from Dad that I'd ever seen about something related to the church or religion.

"What the . . . ?" he exclaimed, catching himself before he said his usual final word, which wouldn't be appropriate on the steps of a church. "How dare they do that?"

He was fat becoming a little hot under his lightly starched collar. Dad was not well educated, and he knew and accepted that as part of life. But he was incredibly proud of what he had been able to put together as a life for himself and his family and this was obviously a major blow to his ego. Our name, hanging out there where everyone could see it. It was a severe public humiliation.

He marched in and had a private -- and I would guess very heated -- conversation with someone in charge of the tithing board. He came back to tell us that they would not remove our name from that week's list of "reminders," and that we would not being going back to St. Paul's.

Not the church. Not ever.

That wound of humiliation was more than Dad could bear and he insisted so firmly that I didn't hear Joan say a word about it in opposition, at least in front of us. Even if we didn't attend church, she did still punish us with rosaries on occasion. She still called us sinners and demons.

I hated St Paul's, and was glad when I learned we weren't going to be attending there any longer, but the public school I moved to wasn't much better in reality. I didn't have any of the right clothes for public school, and not enough in general that I didn't wear the same thing all the time. I was 12 and geeky, tall and painfully skinny with frizzy hair. I didn't feel like I fit in, even though I did have a few good friends. I think every kid feels that way at some point, but the perception was compounded by the fact that life at home was equally dreadful.

Joan and Dad avoided one another like the plague, and when I heard them exchange more than two sentences, they were usually fighting. Dad often went out to hang with Schram and his friends. I had a feeling that Dad was getting into bad business with that Schram. Dad had never really been a scrupulously honest man, making a buck as best he could whenever he saw even a semi-legitimate way to accomplish it. I could remember him bringing home old tires from the dairy farm that still had some tread on them which he sold out of his garage for a few bucks each. I'm not sure if he had actual permission to take them and sell them, or if he had just failed to mention to his employers that he hadn't actually thrown them into the trash.

However, on one morning I woke up very early and crept quietly down the stairs to avoid waking Joan. I wanted to find my cats, of which there were quite a few that lurked around the property which I fed and named, considering them mine. As I turned the corner around the house I came across a number of bills lying on the sidewalk, plastered down with the morning dew. I assumed they must be fake, and later took them in to show Joan.

"Where did you find these?!" she demanded. She saw that I knew nothing of their origin, and looked distant for a moment. "They're real, and I think I know where they came from."

She marched off and confronted Dad, and there was a huge argument about the recovered bills, but I could only hear the yelling, not the words.

Joan's position against Dad was bolstered by the support of her sisters, most of whom outright hated my father and weren't too shy about stating their opinion. The worst of the bunch -- who just happened to be around the most, too -- was Joan's sister, my Aunt Vicky.

Vicky was the sister who had been in the Army, a strange past for a woman in that day and age. She had the build for work, though, tall and broad, with thick legs that pumped like pistons. From Dad, I had learned that those legs were "thunder thighs" and "looked like tree trunks," because they didn't narrow, but stayed one thickness from hip to ankle.

Vicky wore black, cat eye glasses and had awful teeth, which was really saying something in my family. None of the sisters had perfect smiles. Joan had full dentures, and Dad had a partial to fill in for some pulled or missing teeth. But Vicky had fangs, large and prominent front teeth that looked like the overbite of a horse. When she smiled -- which was infrequently -- she had missing teeth on both sides further in the back, which only enhanced the equine image.

She was someone who could stand up to Joan, so strong was her personality. Therefore, Dad was easy prey for her as well.

When her old, pea-green Ford Maverick pulled into our drive and she walked across the lawn to the front door, she'd inevitably see Dad working outside.

"Hello, you ass," she'd say, loud and contemptuous.

"Hello, horse face!" Dad would reply, mock cheerfully.

Then she'd go inside and the sisters' conversation would begin lightly and happily enough, then eventually get louder and louder, each one yelling their point of view at the other as if hers was the only right viewpoint on the planet. I think they respected one another for that ability to argue, for the fact that they were an even match verbally, but that didn't make it any quieter for the rest of us.

I don't know how close they were, but Vicky was the sister who visited us the most. The reason couldn't have been humanitarian, wanting to help take care of the children or something else like that. In fact, we kids were usually pushed out the door. I got a quarter from Dad and walked with Michelle down to the store for candy, hoping Vicky would be gone by the time we got back, although she often wasn't.

They would still be in there, either talking or fighting -- it was hard to tell the difference with those two. From what I heard through the screen door, Vicky liked to sound off about what was wrong with Joan's life, which amounted to what was wrong with my father.

"How do you stand that son of a bitch?" I remember hearing. Other times, she'd start on finances, demanding, "Why can't he take better care of you than this? All these kids and these conditions? He should be ashamed. You should be ashamed."

Dad explained to me that she was so mean and bitter because she never got married. He also said that she was so mean and bitter that no man would marry her, which was kind of the opposite to me, but which he thought equally true. Either way, it didn't matter. He hated her very presence in our home. Dad was elated when in her late 40s Vicky did finally meet and marry someone, an Italian gentleman. The day after the wedding night -- upset about something that had happened between her and the new husband (he had expected intimacy, the lecherous wretch) -- she appeared on our doorstep with a suitcase in hand, having shed her own place in advance of the wedding.

"I don't think so!" Dad yelled from across the lawn, trotting closer to where she stood. "I thought we got rid of you," he complained.

She tried to put on a strong, mean face, but the way she clutched her suitcase made her appear vulnerable.

"Get out of here," he said, unaffected by her exposure.

Joan was at the screen door, where she'd been talking to Vicky. "Frank, you see what happened was . . ."

"I don't care. Doesn't matter," he snapped.

Joan looked at his angry face. "I think you better go," she said to her sister.

Vicky turned and lumbered back to her car. Dad, still livid, kicked a gray cinderblock brick with his work boot. "That's right," he said. "Get out!"

He threw a wrench toward the car's cloud of dust as the Maverick drove away, adding one last word: "And stay out!"

*

The memory of a child is so difficult to read. What they do see and hear, they often don't understand. The truth only becomes clear once they look back from a position of age and experience. So much of my memory is flawed anyway, but so many of these events that I thought were everyday occurrences -- just another bump in the road -- have so much more significance for me now. For me afterward.

I understood that my father took a vacation to Florida, though my memory failed to record exactly how long he was away. I know now it must have been a longer period than it seemed to me at the time although I'm unsure how I could have survived even a coupleof days without him there to support me and protect me from Joan. There were increasingly regular visits from my mother's family. I remember that distinctly because I felt safer when there were other people in the house. She could scold and swat, but she wouldn't strike and maim in front of other eyes.

I remember my father returning and the trinket he brought back as a present for me, a bobble head toy made of sea shells, colored all pink and cream. Michelle got a stuffed A& W Rootbeer bear. He was then back for a significant period of time, though again, I have no idea how long that was.

It's only in retrospect that adults realize that we should have paid attention as children, that there was more happening than meets the kid-sized eye. Only hindsight reveals which moments were the important one versus the mundane, and only then is the true meaning of the stream of events that occur around you every day revealed.

At the time, my imagination could not have even conceived what my life to this point had been leading up to.

## Chapter Five

I loved it when Dad took me to Lowell's dairy for ice cream, with Joan back at home and Michelle already tucked in bed for the night. The drive was long enough that we really got to talk, to have some father-daughter private time. I was 13 now and my long, skinny legs hung over the bench of his bumpy pickup truck.

As I got older I was getting tougher internally and finding my own voice, and the person I felt the most comfortable using that voice with was Dad. He talked about every subject when we were together working or at home, giving me the skinny on anything I wanted to know within reason. He was informal with me, treating me more like an adult than a kid, the sappy and condescending way most grownups do. All of those characteristics made me feel it was okay for me to open up and speak my mind.

With Dad, I could be myself. In Dad's truck, I could bounce on the seat or reach out and change the radio stations, which I did on this particular evening.

He looked over at me and smiled a little. He had a cigarette in his left hand, his left elbow propped up on the open window. It was early September, just a little bit after Labor

Day, and the air was still nice and warm, even at night. During winter when it was cold he'd still smoke but with the windows rolled up, so this arrangement was always better.

We were actually on our way home, I remember. We had gone for ice cream and I had ordered my favorite; black raspberry ice cream in a sugar cone. He always had a cone, too, but I don't remember what flavor of ice cream he preferred it might have been coffee.

"You know she's still doing it," I finally said. "She chased me around today with the strap." It was a subject I brought up often with Dad, more and more as I got older. As usual, he kind of grunted noncommittally.

"What did you do?" he asked, a little malicious glint in his eye. He was always so mischievous himself.

"Nothing!" I protested.

"Nothing?"

"Really, anything I say, she gets mad. It doesn't take anything at all."

He nodded, his face growing sadder as he thought for a moment and seemed to forget to act like everything was okay, the corners of his mouth turning down. He threw the cigarette butt out and put both hands back on the wheel. A few minutes and maybe a mile or two passed before he spoke.

"I know that your mother is a down-right hard person, especially to you kids. Especially to you kids," he repeated. "She just . . ." he trailed off, as if he didn't know how to explain what he was thinking, but it was obvious that the thought he was trying to express made him frustrated, sad, and even angry. "But I want you to know that everything is going to be fine now," he continued. "Everything is going to be better for you and your sister from now on."

I snorted through my nose, a gesture I probably learned from him. As many times as I'd brought up the subject of Joan and the pain she caused, he'd just as often said something similar. But nothing ever changed.

"Oh, really?" I asked. "What are you going to do? How is it going to be better?"

He was quiet, looking forward. He didn't look very lighthearted now. Instead, he seemed very calm and sincere.

"It just is," he said. "I promise."

He glanced over at me, directly in the eye with intent and gave me a little smile, the kind that tried to drag a smile out of me as well. As always, it worked and I smiled, relaxing a little bit into his promise of change -- even if I didn't wholly believe it. There was something different about his manner this time, however, and I wondered if he had obtained some sort of ability or talisman that he could employ over the evil queen of our life story. He was more sincere in his assurance than usual, and it was noticeable in the way he spoke.

We drove the rest of the way home as usual, talking about nothing much.

*

The next day was a Friday -- Friday, September 10, 1976. I was in school as on any weekday, sitting at a desk or reading a textbook, completely unaware of anything going on beyond a foot in front of my own nose. Therefore, I could not have seen or heard what transpired at home. The facts that I know come from the newspaper reports of that day, which I can neither confirm or deny as truthful, but simply state as if for the record, as if for some invisible jury, though no verdict will ever be handed down.

At about 8:50 a.m., and for unknown reasons, Dad was home at the house on Blackstone Street. This was completely at odds with his normal schedule, which would have found him at work, a 45-minute drive away. Friday was payday, so perhaps that had something to do with it.

Money certainly had to play some part. There was a stack of about $400 in cash lying on the kitchen table. This was not an amount of money to be thrown around easily in my family.

The newspaper reports that Dad approached Joan and said, "Can I have a minute of your time?" There's no source for that information -- there were no witnesses other than Joan and Frank -- as well as no explanation of why Frank would talk so formally, or what he wanted to ask her.

There was very little conversation apparently, and the report says that Joan turned away from him to go take a shower and get dressed. When she returned, Dad again asked for "a minute of her time." However this time, he was holding a .22-caliber bolt-action rifle: a long, lean gun with a barrel the length of a man's arm. Dad had always had guns around the house. I can recall several handguns of his, but this particular rifle was unfamiliar to me.

Seeing the gun, Joan screamed and ran for the side kitchen door. The first bullet pierced the aluminum door frame. Shell casing No. 1 was found on the kitchen floor.

Joan continued to run along the side of the house toward the street. Dad emerged from the same door, sighted along the rifle and shot again. Shell No. 2 was found in the side yard.

Joan reached the front yard, angling toward the nearest neighbor, the Davidsons. Mr. Davidson was welding in his front yard and Mrs. Davidson was indoors. Dad tracked back through the interior of the house to the front door where he stood on the steps and again took aim. He shot again, and shell No. 3 was recovered from the grass.

Mr. Davidson saw the third shot fired. Mrs. Davidson only heard it.

Two of the three bullets hit Joan, both in the back. One bullet shattered a rib as it exited from her chest, then lodged in her right arm. The second bullet shattered after entering her back, splintering both bullet and bone.

Bleeding heavily and stumbling, Joan continued toward the Davidsons'. It's unclear whether she collapsed in the front entry of their home after knocking or while she was still outside.

Either way, her only words were, "Frank just shot me."

Along with another neighbor, Mrs. Foster, the Davidsons bundled Joan in a blanket and got her into the Davidsons' car. Mrs. Davidson meanwhile called the police to report the shooting, but before the police arrived, the neighbors and Joan were on their way to the Woonsocket hospital.

From newspaper accounts, my neighborhood was perceived by others in town in a different way than I had always defined it. It was said to be working class and populated with relatively isolationist families that didn't often interact. One officer stated, "To show you what kind of a neighborhood it is, and how typical, when Mrs. Foster ran to help Mr. Davidson, it was the first time the two had ever really met." The newspaper called thc neighborhood "a typical, tranquil, residential area, comprised of working people who seldom bother with each other."

Apparently, in the car, Mrs. Foster remarked, "What an awful way to meet one another."

Sometime between when Joan collapsed with the Davidsons and the police arrived, Dad shot himself twice in the chest with the same rifle, which needed to be cocked after each shot and, again, was the length of his entire arm. It seems an awkward procedure for one shot, let alone two, but he managed it somehow -- apparently. He was still alive when the first officers arrived on scene, but only for a few moments.

Dad died in the hallway between the living room and kitchen. He lay facedown, wearing his matching work shirt and pants. To his left sat his untied work boots, neatly placed in the corner as if waiting for their well known feet to return. On Dad's feet instead were his house slippers, the soles blotted with stepped-in blood.

Death was confirmed by a state medical examiner. Two Catholic priests arrived, presumably to administer the last rites of the church. Also at the scene, for reasons unknown, were a town administrator and a town selectman. The latter was a cousin of mine, Dad's nephew, the son of one of his sisters.

Information that emerged in later days included the fact that about an hour before the shooting the Blackstone police received a call about a domestic disturbance, though no connection was ever established between that call and the events that unfolded at my family home.

In fact, one of the officers on the scene called the shooting "unbelievable," saying, "They might have been having a family problem but this department never once had to go to their home on a domestic complaint call."

The family problems to which he was referring, according to the newspaper on the day of the event were that "police believe Mrs. Dubois had a restraining order issued against her husband and would not allow him to enter the home."

The next day's report changed the story:

> "The couple had been estranged but [Dad] recently moved back in with his wife and three children. The children were in school when the shootings occurred . . . Calls are already coming in at the station from townspeople offering to help

the three children. Last night the children stayed with an aunt and uncle."

Only parts of these assertions can I personally confirm. I was at school when it all happened. I stayed the night at my aunt and uncle's house. These things I recall, but everything else is a blur of fear, surprise, agony and supposition.

*

I was called to the main office of my school to find my Uncle Jack, my mother's only brother still alive, waiting there for me. He was holding his coat in his hands and said, "There's been an accident. Your father is dead, and your mother is in critical condition in the ICU at the hospital." He was always a rather matter of fact man, probably a condition of growing up among so many loud and assertive women, but even now he seemed to maintain precise control of his emotions.

*Your father is dead. My father? My father is dead.*

Dad was dead, really and actually dead. My first reaction was one of disbelief, of feeling that I'd stepped into a scene from someone else's life. I didn't say a word, and all my facial muscles went limp and numb. My mind, on the other hand, was buzzing.

*How is that possible?* I thought, stunned. *One day he's eating ice cream and joking and his heart is beating. He can't really be dead. He has a goofy smile and wavy hair and big, strong hands, and dead people don't have any of those things. A real person like that can't just die, because then I'd never see him again, never speak to him again. I have to at least get to talk to him one more time, right?*

From that moment on -- being told the news that Dad was dead and Joan had been shot and was in the hospital -- a break happened within me, a snapped cord that connected the reality of the outside world with my inner life. My real self took a step back into my head, as if in doing so I could add a layer of protection. She still looked out of my eyes, heard from my ears, but was at a removed pace from the real world. My memories are crinkly and unfocused, as if I was walking around packed in tissue paper, labeled "handle with care."

From school, I was whisked straight to the hospital where they'd taken Joan. All of her sisters and Jack were there, crowded into a hallway waiting room with a row of plastic chairs. Their faces were in various states of grief. Some looked mildly damp and humid with tears wiped away. The more violently upset were convulsing with sobs, hands clutching tissues held to their mouths, tears streaming down cheeks or eyes squeezed tightly shut against the world.

I sat next to Michelle on one of the chairs. We held hands, linking all 5fingers between all 5of the other's, tight and solid. We were somewhat left alone and apart from the others. In such situations families often break off into units I've found, cliques perhaps, parents gathering and comforting their own brood, kids seeking out moms and dads. I don't think most of the families there had really processed the fact that our parents weren't here for us we were alone, were not going to be here, and they might have stepped into that role for the two of us. But no one did.

I can't say that I joined in the tears of the family. In fact, the primary thought that ran through my head as I stared at the hospital wall was: *It's over. It's actually over. Dad did finally end it, once and for all. He did it.*

Quickly following, my second thought questioned whether my primary one made me a bad person. My mother was in critical condition, rushed into emergency surgery. *And I'm not sorry, not one little, tiny bit. Does that make me evil? Am I going to hell like she always threatened?*

But because I was at that physical remove, rattling around inside my head, I took that thought and crammed it in a box, put it away in a deep, dark corner where I wouldn't have to think about it. There was an ache in my chest for Dad, a sensation like a dark hole in my ribs which was pulling, pressing and threatening to pull me inside out. It was all I could do to breathe, and so the thoughts were just going to have to wait.

There was a lot of chaos in the hospital. The doctor came out and talked to the adults. At one point, the aunts began wailing at the news he delivered. I heard the word cardiac arrest and I knew what that meant from watching television.

Joan was dying. Dad had killed Joan.

*Thank you, Dad. I love you too. But . . . now you're gone too. What will I do without you?*

My reaction to the news didn't seem appropriate somehow, apparently, because one of my aunts chastised me for being cold about my dear mother's condition. *My dear mother* . . . I couldn't even bring myself to think of her as my mother as she lay dying in the hospital. She was a monster -- a baby beater, a bloodthirsty demon whose only pleasure was inflicting pain and injuries on those weaker than herself. My only feelings about my dear mother had been limited to surviving around her, and keeping my defenseless baby sister out of her evil clutches. Yes, my dear mother . . . perhaps I failed to demonstrate the appropriate level of grief at her demise. I could grant my aunt that.

Soon after we received the news about Joan's cardiac arrest Michelle and I were bundled out of the hospital and to Aunt Roz's house, where we were given food and a place to lie down, but no further information.

When I came into the kitchen for dinner, the evening paper was on the table. Aunt Roz had her back turned to me, hadn't heard me come in, or she might have prevented what happened next. On the front page was the inch-high headline: *Man shoots wife, kills self.* And then there was a graphic photo of my father's body, lying face down on the familiar linoleum floor of our family home. The caption read, "The body of Frank H. Dubois, 48, lies in the blood spattered hallway of his home." It was pretty graphic for a small town newspaper. I later learned that a news photographer sneaked past the police and snatched the photo before they could catch him.

I remember certain vivid details of that photo: the bottoms of Dad's slippered feet, dark with blood, the slippers making him seem so vulnerable. His hands were at his sides, palms up toward the ceiling. Those were definitely his hands, his strong and oil stained hands that I'd seen at work so many times. It was at that moment the enormity of what happened that day struck me. It sank in then that something awful and violent had taken place in my house, that my dad was dead, and that I would neither live in my house or have my dad with me ever again. It was at that moment that I knew my life was never going to be the same.

I made a gagging sound in my throat, half sob and half fear, and Roz turned around to see me. She grabbed the paper off the table and out of my view, but it was still in her hand. She gave the photo a nasty glare and said, in a violent whisper, "Disgusting pig. He deserves what he got."

The outburst may have been unconscious, because she then quickly looked up at me, back down at the paper and threw it out of sight, or perhaps even threw it away. Though I wouldn't see the image again until I was an adult, it was seared in my memory. Dad stiff and dead, and my aunt calling him a pig.

I didn't understand why she would say such a thing. There must have been more going on than I realized at that age for her to have such a strong feeling about the man that I idolized. *Who was she to say such things?* I thought. *She didn't know him like I did. She's never treated me half as well as he did. She wasn't half the person he was.*

I polished my memories of Dad in my head until they positively glowed, as if he'd always had a halo over his head, lit up with his love for me. Then I slept in Roz's uncomfortable guest bed in a house that smelled of fried food and stale cigarette smoke.

*

A few days passed and Roz took us by the house to pick up some of our things. My sister Hope was at the house for part of our visit as well as my other aunts, Carley and Vicky.

There was a massive blood stain on the floor where Dad had lain. Blood was also splashed on the walls and windows. Muddy feet had tramped in and out of the house and everywhere were the signs of the police investigation: crime scene tape, cameras, paperwork, evidence bags. The window in the kitchen had been broken, probably shot out, and the door jamb was splintered.

*Man, Joan would have been so mad at this mess.* I almost giggled at the thought.

For a while, I remember that I helped my older sister Hope in cleaning up some of the disaster. I did it robotically, because I was told, and had no emotion about it.

Despite all that was intensely disturbing about returning to that house, not very much was different that I could tell. All our clothes were still hanging in their appointed places in the closet, all the shoes lined up in place. We grabbed a suitcase or two already full of clothes, snapped them shut and brought them downstairs. I learned later that one of the aunts gathered up a few of the more personal trinkets of my parents for us kids to keep, finding a few of them squirreled away in my suitcase a few days afterward.

We returned to Roz's house for another night, and that evening Michelle and I were sat down to a very somber and severe lecture from the aunts. They took turns, speaking over one another but repeating the same message.

"This is a horrible, horrible thing that your father did. He was obviously a severely disturbed, evil and hateful man. A sinner," I was told. "Your mother is still hanging by a thread and we need you to pray for her recovery and her soul."

I didn't.

"But the point is that everything changes now because what happened was a very big deal, for us and for the whole town. But because it was such a big deal, it's very important that as far as this family goes, it didn't happen."

*My father is dead, Joan is dying.*

"It never happened, and if someone asks you about what happened, you deny it. Do you understand?"

I didn't.

"It's bad enough that we all lived through something awful like this, something so evil that your evil father did. But we will not bring it into the future. We will not talk about. Never."

*Fine,* I thought. *Another family secret, another family shame.* I was well used to that kind of thing, and especially now, I was getting better and better about taking thoughts and emotions and whole events and burying them deep in my subconscious where they couldn't hurt me.

# Chapter Six

I spent one more night in town, at my friend Peggy's house. Michelle stayed somewhere else, but I wasn't told where.

Time became a blur for me. The world became a blur. I have little memory of what transpired over the days and weeks that followed. Time passed on and on, and unknown to me, or just blocked out by my mind, Joan began to heal from her wounds.

We moved out of the house in Blackstone and it was sold to my 7th grade science teacher, Tom Fisher. He and his family must have picked it up for a bargain since it was the house of death and mayhem. They stayed there through my adult years and 15 years ago I returned to the home to see my old room. Tom had left my little hiding area the exact way it was from when I was a little girl. The room had changed because he had boys, but he left my hiding place the same. He gave me a light and told me to go inside. My heart raced and pounded and being much taller I had to duck down to avoid hitting the ceiling beams with my head. All of my drawings on the walls were intact and my safe little place quickly calmed me down.

My memories are foggy over exactly what transpired next, being uncertain until I did research to ensure I had my facts straight. We were in Milford and Joan had volunteers that took care of her. I ran away to get away from her. I stayed everywhere and anywhere I could so I wouldn't have to be with her. Michelle was much older now and could basically fend for herself. I had a job at the local McDonalds and babysat when needed. The few things that do stick in my mind from this time was Joan telling me I wouldn't be a virgin if I used tampons and she refused to buy them for me. Forced to buy my own I had to spend what little money I made getting necessities. At one point I became very ill and Joan refused to get me help. Michelle was my only source of communication as I refused to talk to Joan. I had become so ill that I told Michelle I thought I was going to die. It wasn't until this point that Joan finally had someone take me to the hospital where I was diagnosed with a severe case of mononucleosis and my spleen was about to rupture. I was put into the pediatric ward due to my age and I remember telling the night nurse not to let Joan into my room if she somehow found a way to get there.

*

While I was walking home from my friend Lynn's house one night I was attacked and raped by a man that had followed me. I was hit repeatedly with a rock and was left in the woods to die, bleeding and terrified. I was disoriented but did manage to make it back to the apartment in Milford. Joan immediately accused me of asking for it, saying that that I was a whore and a slut.

For the first time I fought back. Maybe it was the pent up anger from all the years, maybe it was the fact she was still around and not dead, or maybe it was the fresh wounds on my face and body and her stupid *holier than thou* attitude that I somehow asked to be raped? Whatever it was I didn't hold back. I slammed her small, damaged body against the wall and slapped her across the face. I then pushed her to the floor and told her she was worthless.

It was shortly thereafter I was declared a ward of the state. I had no idea what that meant as the gavel was lowered on the decision. I simply found myself on an uncomfortable wooden bench, typical government building issue, with my suitcase next to me, one hand threaded through its handle. She had given me up to the state. She had given up her rights to me and was no longer my mother. I remember the judge reprimanding her for the decision but my caseworker had shared with him it was the best thing that could have ever happened to me. Dad had failed in his attempt to expunge her from my life; to take away the constant and unwarranted abuse. He failed because she lived, and it was still going on.

Most strangely, some kind of state representative appeared and safety pinned a square index card on my shirt. In neat, typed letters, the card said my name, my age and some number I didn't recognize.

I was told I was waiting to be taken someplace else.

"Where?" I asked.

"To the Milford Assistance Program."

"What's that?"

"That's the place where you will be living now that you're a ward of the state." I was silent because I didn't know precisely what the phrase meant. "That means that because your parents can't take care of you, the state is going to from now on at this new place, where there are other kids just like you that they take care of."

*That's it*, I thought. *I have no parents! And I'm going to an orphanage just like Joan always threatened she would send me.*

"The orphanage?" I asked.

"No, no," she was quick to clarify. "Being a state ward just means that you don't have family to take care of you, but as a state ward we make sure we find people who will."

I'm sure whoever that person was that they had wait with me, she was trying to be comforting. It didn't work, however. Instead, I had a tornado of questions in my head. I had aunts who could have taken me in. I had grown-up sisters, too. Granted, they had young families of their own they needed to care for. But the aunts? Didn't I have family?

I shook my head and sighed, remembering their talk of Dad as an evil sinner, a horrible man. They knew I didn't believe that. They knew I didn't like them. Perhaps they even knew I hated Joan. I wasn't surprised that they didn't want anything to do with me. They thought I was evil like Dad. They knew that part of me had celebrated my mother's attack. Maybe I was evil.

"Where's Michelle? What about my sister Michelle?" I asked, my voice a little panicked. I hadn't seen her all day, perhaps longer.

"Oh, I'm sorry, dear," the state representative said. "She's not allowed any contact with you. She can't go to Milford with you."

This was the most stunning revelation of all, like severing a living part of my body. My Michelle, my beloved little sister Michelle. She was only nine years old and was not going to be living with me. I hadn't seen her, wouldn't see her. The thought cleaved my heart like an axe and I wept all through the car ride to what they called being a state ward. I knew that was just fancy language. What they were really doing was sending me to an orphanage, what Joan had wanted since the day of my birth.

I was definitely not going to pray for Joan's soul.

*

The Milford Assistance Program, or MAP, was a county-run program for unwanted or wayward teens located in or around the town of Milford, east of Blackstone by about 20 miles. The edifice was stark and uninviting, more like a commercial place of business than a home. Made of light brick, it was a sharp square where all the visible windows were barred. Inside, I was led to a bench where I was supposed to wait for someone. The sticky vinyl seat cushion was bolted to the metal bench, and the metal bench was bolted to the floor.

I sat and looked again down at the card pinned to my shirt. The hallway felt like an empty bus station as I sat there with my suitcase. The big picture of how the process went is so hazy to me, but the details are stark. I remember the ticking of the clock as I waited. I was very hungry and didn't know the last time I had eaten. My mind drifted to Dad, but then I squinted my eyes shut hard on the thought.

*No, we're not thinking about that. Put it away.*

Instead, I kept my mind purposely blank and painless, listening to the ticking of the clock.

A woman approached, a woman I eventually came to think of as the Brown Lady. It wasn't difficult to see the reason for the name I had assigned her: she was dressed head to toe in brown, from the brown flats on her feet and her brown tights to the modest skirt and the collared shirt, or perhaps it was more of a light jacket. It seemed like a sort of uniform to me, like I'd seen people from the Salvation Army or candy stripers wear. I can't remember her face, but can conjure up her brown form easily.

After her introduction, I asked the most important question again. "Where is my sister? Where is my sister Michelle?"

She may have had some paperwork with her which she consulted or she may have just known, but she replied, "She's too young for this facility, Lorijane."

I didn't understand what was going on and no one had any satisfactory answers for me, so the questions just whirred on, becoming the background music of my life at Milford.

First, the staff had to make sure I wasn't physically contaminated or infected. My hair and body were checked for lice. I opened my mouth for a nurse to see my teeth and tonsils. My temperature was taken.

Then I was introduced into the general population of kids. I was tall and skinny at 14, but there were older and taller kids there, probably close to the age of liberation at 18. There were smaller kids too, as young as six years old, I would guess, so I couldn't understand why Michelle wasn't allowed there with me. It was a group of mostly white kids, which is typical for that part of the country, especially at that time, and all of them were a little ragged. No one was downright dirty and no one's clothes were in tatters. Everyone was just a little worn around the edges.

That could also maybe be attributed to the bad lighting. With the combination of the bars and streaks on the glass, the light from the windows was dim. Everything that could be stolen was bolted down, including our beds, which were cots with scratchy wool blankets I imagined were similar to those in Army barracks. Perhaps that was where they had come from, Army surplus. The food served in the cafeteria was horrendous, making even Joan's cooking seem better in comparison.

I was in and out of the Milford Assistance Program for several years, so I got used to the routine. The number one rule was to not speak to any of the adults unless you were asked a question. Number two was not to make trouble among the other kids. The most important rule in my book was that I had to take care of myself. No one else was going to do it for me.

For instance, when I'd first opened my suitcase upon getting to Milford, I found several items that someone from the family (one of my sisters, perhaps) had obviously wanted me to keep. Among the first I saw was a wooden tray that I recognized immediately. It was the tray on which Dad placed all his personal items at the end of the day, including his watch, comb, wallet, money clip and keys. The watch or the money clip would have been more sentimental than the tray on which they rested, but I was thankful for it nonetheless. My rosary was tucked into an interior pocket of the suitcase, and I also found a few small dolls and figurines, some photos, a couple of records stuck in the back sleeve and the bobble head that Dad had brought back for me from Florida, covered in shells.

Every single item was stolen over the course of a few months by other kids, teaching me why the staff thought it necessary to nail everything else down.

As time went by, it didn't seem to matter to me. At that age and in that time period, no one really talked about depression, so I don't know if that's what I was experiencing or not. I only know that I felt detached, unmoored from reality. My brain seemed to turn off, bored by the mundane routine of everything. But at the same time, I continued to have some unnamed need I wasn't able to identify. I couldn't put my finger on exactly what it was. I had no house, no sister, no parents, no cousins, no familiar school. Then, there were no possessions. *Oh, well . . . What does it matter?* I could still work up feelings of possession about things of the distant past, like the prized rubber ball I used to win at jacks with during school recess that I hid in my desk, but nothing in this life -- this life afterward -- seemed concrete enough that I could hang on to it. And yet I yearned for . . . something.

I heard nothing from my family, even though I was now just five towns over from what had been my family home in Blackstone. I had no phone numbers or access to a phone, so I had no way of reaching out to my relatives as they remained silent. I was told that Michelle had been placed in Carter House in Pawtucket, Rhode Island. Carter was a place for wayward and disobedient children. At least I knew she was safe—it had to be safer than being under Joan's "care," anyway. No one came to see me and no one wrote. Eventually, I just accepted that MAP was a place for bad kids and the fact that my family had abandoned me in this place with no news confirmed that they agreed. I was a bad person. No one wanted me.

In Milford, there was a routine in terms of who stayed and who went back out into the world. We got up every morning and tidied ourselves, because that gave us the best chance to impress. Then when the nearest adult told us to, we'd stand in front of a particular wall of windows where we couldn't see out, but obviously visitors could see in. Potential foster parents came trooping by to take our measure and decide if they wanted to take any particular child home with them.

I did have several of those visitors open their houses to me. Most of them didn't open their hearts.

The first family to take me in was an older couple, at least in their 60s, with a very cold demeanor. They gave me a bedroom and list of chores, and told me they were working on getting me enrolled in school. But the weeks dragged on and the latter never materialized. They basically just wanted extra help around the house, and indeed, the list of duties they gave me every day filled all of my hours until bedtime. I felt like Cinderella . . . without any prospects.

Every MAP kid was given a phone number and secret pocket money when they went to live with a new family. They told us to keep very quiet about this pocket money, because it was to be used in an emergency to call MAP and ask for rescue. When it became clear that the old couple had no intention of sending me to school or of allowing me to live a somewhat normal life I took my secret pocket change to the bar across the street. I used the pay phone to tell the state representatives that the couple wasn't putting me in school but was using me as slave labor, and I quickly found myself back in Milford, the second worst place I could imagine.

Next I was in what I thought was a regular foster home, where they took in kids with some regularity. But the place was filthy and disgusting, the opposite of the clean at the older couple's home. In the end, they were apparently on the waiting list for a boy and were only dealing with me out of necessity -- because I was "just a girl" -- until a boy could be sent. He was. And I went.

Every time such a transition occurred at any foster home, it was the Brown Lady who would arrive on the scene with her flat and sensible coffee shoes. The uniform became a sign that someone was coming or going, which was sometimes a good sign and sometimes a bad one. It was good when she took you away from troublesome families, and it was bad when you were the one who was troublesome and you were being sent away again, *return to sender*. The Brown Lady drove a large station wagon that could fit six kids, all of us sliding around on the big vinyl bench seats.

There were smaller, shorter assignments, too. I had a temporary home with a family that had another girl about my age. I tagged along with her to school for the time I was there, but there didn't seem much point in it. I didn't have the books, I wouldn't be graded on the assignments. I'd soon be back at the MAP anyway. A few other times I recall weekend stints, where a family would take you in for a few days to give you break from the institutional life, and let you relax a little. I also spent several spells of many weeks at a time in larger group foster homes, where up to 10 kids could be at one time. At least it was smaller and had more privacy than Milford.

Throughout my time at the Milford Assistance Program I periodically met with some sort of administrator. I think they called it therapy, but it wasn't the type of therapy that I probably needed. The adult asked mostly about my behavior and how I was functioning, and told me about any upcoming moves that might be scheduled. I constantly asked about Michelle, but no one ever knew any information about my sister.

The Milford nightmare only ended when I met Ruby.

*

Ruby Bickford was a middle-aged woman with blue eyes, short, bleached blonde hair and a smile shining with straight, white teeth. She was plump, but in a very friendly way, her bust and belly bouncing when she laughed. And according to her face, which had crinkly laugh lines that made her appear even more accessible and nice, she must have laughed often.

She had once been married and had two kids from that marriage; a daughter Barbara who was a year older than me, and a son Dylan who was a year younger than me. Sometime a while back -- it must have been long ago, because it seemed like old, uninteresting news -- her husband had run off and left her a single mother. When I met her, she was working at the Wrentham State School, a facility for adult mentally handicapped persons, and lived on a large piece of horse property with the kids and Ingrid, a fifty-something woman with downs syndrome that she'd met at work and taken into her home.

It seemed I was to be the home's newest addition, the latest stray cat.

The administration at the Milford Assistance Program had given me a choice in the matter, asking if it was a situation I wanted to try. Once I found out that Ruby lived on a farm with 8 horses, 5 dogs and a couple of rabbits, I was sold on the proposition. I'd always loved animals.

From the first moment I arrived, I may have sometimes been disoriented, but I never regretted the choice. The MAP representative drove me up to an old, rambling farmhouse where the paint was not peeling, but just old enough to add character, looking like the windows could wink at you. In the distance was a barn and I saw at least one horse out in the fields. We came into the main level, where there was a farm kitchen and a living room, the master bedroom to one side. We talked for about an hour before the representative left and I was alone with Ruby. She wore a simple short-sleeved shirt and a smile from ear to ear as she showed me around what she called "your new home."

One spiral staircase led upstairs to Dylan's room and a guestroom, and my bedroom was to be on the topmost, third floor, where Ingrid and Barbara also had private bedrooms. I immediately loved it. My room had pitched ceilings sloping down to a dormer window overlooking the fields. It was adorably tiny. The furnishings were simple -- nothing but a bed, a desk and a dresser -- but it felt quaint and fun, like something out of a novel.

I was thrilled. When I turned around to Ruby, I was sporting the most genuine smile I had dug up in years. I had a feeling she wanted to hug me, to smush me right into her chubby arms and ample bosom, but I was still an unknown quantity, a skittish colt.

When she opened her mouth through her smile to talk, however, it became immediately obvious that this jolly woman, while open and friendly, was also someone I didn't want to mess around with.

"So this is how it works around here," she began. "We have a set of house rules and you will follow them."

Her eyes met mine with the last words, stressing that this was not a request.

"Everyone helps out around the house, and everyone helps out with the horses, so you're going to have to learn to do that. I'm told you agreed to that," she said.

I nodded.

"You will get up in the morning at seven. You will not miss the school bus. I'll show you where the stop is," she continued. "After school, you will be given a set of chores just like the other kids, to do until five o'clock, when you start on your homework. Dinner is at six o'clock, and you help with the washing up, and then you finish your homework. Is all that understood?"

Again, I nodded, wondering if I had exchanged one prison for another one. At least this one had a window where I could begin each morning with a sunlit view over pastureland and horses.

"Understood, yes. But it will also all be followed?" Again, her eyes probed mine, searching for signs of trouble.

"Yes, Ma'am," I said, using the polite form of address that had been drilled into me over the last few years.

Her smile widened. "Call me Ruby," she said. "Welcome home."

*

It may sound strange, but that first conversation is one of my favorite memories of Ruby Ruby had a unique style of communication, speaking very fast and getting directly to the point without any dilly dallying. It was part of her personality to be frank and honest, and to expect the same from everyone else. She was the kindest person I've ever met. She worked with the handicapped, and had opened her heart and home to Ingrid and me. Ruby wouldn't hurt a fly. All the horses on the property were rescued race horses, animals that had outlived their usefulness at the track that otherwise would have been put down, sent to the dog food factory.

Ruby smoked long, white cigarettes, and occasionally enjoyed a beer in the sun with Tom, a hired man who helped out around the farm. She often took care of Tom's son in her spare time. She also had very unusual friends, one of her closest being a former prostitute. I remember Ruby once taking me to visit a man in prison that she corresponded with. She said that everybody deserved a second chance. Much as I suspected the first time I met her, Ruby gave tremendously tight and affectionate bear hugs. It was the only kind of hug she had in her.

But at the same time she was sweet and kind, she was rigid and disciplined about what was right and wrong, was acceptable and unacceptable, and you didn't want to cross her.

Strangely, I found that I thrived on the structure that Ruby imposed on my new life on her horse farm. The routine kept me busy and focused on action, not constantly brooding over my losses. I was productive and happy, and the strict schedule and rules -- which did flex somewhat over time as we got to know each other -- actually made me feel safe.

It was odd, to be living in a house as a family again, but with all these strangers that weren't my family. Her two kids were very nice. They both played the piano, which was a delightful novelty for me. Ingrid, too, was often fun to be around. She cracked jokes with us kids and acted as an unofficial babysitter when Ruby worked the night shift. In truth, we all just looked after one another. It was a nice feeling. I was even enjoying high school.

In the morning before school, Ruby had a particular way of waking us kids up. She knocked on my door and opened it, then said, "You have three seconds to open your eyes before I turn this light on."

I would always hurry to obey and open my eyes. I hated being woken by that kind of bright light, which is often how it worked at the Milford Assistance Program, although Ruby couldn't have known that.

One morning after I'd been there a few weeks, I came down to what had become my favorite breakfast: oatmeal with extra maple syrup in it. It was just Ruby and I in the kitchen at that point, and she took the opportunity to have a serious chat with me.

"Lorijane, I know you don't know me," said Ruby, "but I want you to know that you can trust me. I honestly care about you, and I want you to fit in to this family. I want you to be one of my kids."

"But I'm a teenager," I said. It was the only thing that came to mind.

She laughed. "I know," she said. "I mean that I really want to see this work out. I really want to see you be happy."

She put her hand over mine. I was touched, but I had no idea how to respond to her unexpected announcement. She seemed to know that, giving my hand a little squeeze and turning back to her morning chores.

Gradually, I learned everything I needed to know about doing my part to take care of the horses. I knew how to clean out the stalls, how to tell when they should be fed and when to call a farrier when they began to outgrow their shoes. I took the horses out one by one to the walker -- the big metal carousel wheel where you exercise them in a circle. Because they were older and former racers, many of the horses had special needs and the vet was on the property often. On one occasion, the whole family and the doctor were out in the barn at two o'clock in the morning trying to get one of the female horses to her feet so the doctors could fix something wrong in her stomach. We pushed and heaved, but nothing worked, and the horse ended up dying.

The farm environment suited my tomboy nature, surrounded as I was by turtles, snakes, frogs and all this other cool stuff that fascinated me. I had learned that the first thing a toad does when you pick it up is urinate, but once it's finished, that's it. They are great to hold. I was interested to such a degree that I sometimes took animals back into the house, up to my room. The toad would just hang out with me on the desk while I did my homework. However, I did sometimes forget about them and, whether in the middle of the afternoon or the middle of the night, you'd hear someone shriek and then start to yell, "Lorijane!"

At times, I knew that Ruby's daughter Barbara got resentful of my presence in the house, me being another girl of her approximate age. I once overheard Barbara talking to her mom about it in the kitchen.

"Why did you bring this other girl into the house?" she asked. "Why do you need another daughter?"

Ruby replied, "I didn't need her. She needed me. She needs us."

I was so touched by her insight into my character and needs that tears came to my eyes, and I crept back upstairs to my room so no one would see me cry.

Just like at other foster homes, the Brown Lady or one of the other Milford representatives would stop by every once in a while to check up on how I was doing. That basically meant they wanted to make sure I was behaving myself, and their feigned concern annoyed me.

After a few months, another such visitor came to the door. I was in the room behind Ruby when she answered the door.

In reply to the woman asking how I was doing and to be let in, Ruby said, "She's doing just fine."

The woman attempted to continue, but Ruby went on.

"No, she's doing fine. You don't need to worry about her at all."

She continued saying that until the Milford lady finally assented and went her way. It was soon after that incident when Ruby began the formal process of adopting me as her daughter.

I was given a new mom at the age of 16.

*

Ruby noticed that I liked to draw and bought me an easel and art supplies to keep in my room. As I progressed through high school she fanned the flame of that passion by supporting me in all my budding artistic endeavors, her encouragement giving me the strength to expect more from myself than I ever had before. I was part of a highly prestigious advanced art program and took part in many art shows and competitions.

Her praise made me blush, and I said I hoped I would make her proud. She replied, "You make me proud just by being you." Indeed, I had not heard that kind of positive talk since Dad's death.

Much as she wished, I did find myself becoming part of this family of strangers. I no longer thought of myself as abandoned or unwanted, or somehow evil. In fact, memories of my life in Blackstone started to fade from my everyday life. At times, I even forgot -- or more accurately was not constantly thinking -- that I had a little sister out there that I missed with all my heart.

When I was a senior in high school, Ruby came into my room with a newspaper clipping and slipped it onto my desk in front of me. I was shocked when I read the headline and realized she had clipped out the obituary of a man named Armand. Armand had been my godfather, way back, once upon a time in that other life.

I gasped. *How did Ruby know that this man was my godfather, that his death would be important to me? Did she . . . How much did she know about me . . . about my family and what was going on with them?*

Ruby didn't tell me where she'd found the obituary or how she knew this man was connected to me. She just placed a gentle hand on my shoulder and left me to my thoughts.

My family was just on the other side of the state of Massachusetts -- an hour's drive really. For years, I had no contact with anyone in my family, and now I wondered if Ruby had.

I suppose I never thought of the fact that Ruby must know the whole story of my family. She would have been told everything about me by the Milford Assistance Program before she even brought me into her home as a foster child, and she would have been the legal guardian of everything -- all my records -- after the adoption.

I had buried the past so deep that I thought the rest of the world had too.

*"It never happened, and if someone asks you about what happened, you deny it. Do you understand?" my aunt's voice echoed through my mind.*

My life was going so well. I was succeeding at school, to the point that I earned a partial art scholarship to college. I had decided to defer the scholarship for a while, instead enlisting in the Navy for four years. They would help pay for college after I gave them my contracted time, and besides, Dad had been a Navy man.

Now, the past came rushing back up to the surface of my mind from where it was lurking on a lower, subconscious level, forcing me to re-open that book. Forcing me to confront the most important of the old questions.

*Where was Michelle?*

*

The only thing I was able to discover about Michelle was that she was at Cariter's House, she had spent almost five years in that awful facility for trouble-making girls. I began to send her letters that were returned unopened, missives of my thoughts and feelings for her that failed to connect. That year when I was 18, however, I had other tools at my disposal.

I had friends, and specifically, I had a friend with a car.

Cariter's House wasn't too long of a drive and when you parked out front, it was possible to see the big, open yard where the girls came out for recreation time. It was about seven o'clock in the evening, just after dinner, and all at once, the stream of kids came through a door and into the open air.

I felt so amazingly lucky, to have not seen my sister in years and then to have this opportunity where she could be right in front of me, face to face. From the picture in my mind I tried to project her image to the real, living sister I had missed so much.

I left my friend in the car and went running up to the chain link fence around the yard. The uniform white shirts of all the girls were difficult to see through; they all looked the same. So I began to shout.

"Michelle! Michelle! Michelle!"

Some of the girls turned to look at me like I was a crazy person, but I didn't care. Besides, the effort was soon rewarded when from 20 yards away, I saw a head turn. Her familiar chin. Her memorable eyes. It was Michelle!

"Lorijane?" she called, at first confused. Then her face burst into a smile and she ran over to greet me at the fence. Her hair was quite a bit longer than I remembered. Her legs were so long. She was so incredibly tall, as if someone had stretched the child I once knew. She was a young woman now, and she was beautiful.

"Well, it's about time you came and saw me," she said, still smiling. She pushed her hair behind her ear.

I laughed. I saw that she'd developed an attitude along with all the other physical changes.

"My letters came back. No one would tell me anything about you or the family or anything," I explained quickly. She watched me for a moment. "So, how awful is it in here?"

"It's strict. It's all, 'Do this, and don't do that,'" she said.

"But they don't hit you?" I looked for clarification.

She shook her head. *Thank God,* I thought. *At least she's been safe.*

"And where are you then? In foster care, I know," said Michelle.

I nodded. I have a new mom, and she's just wonderful," I explained. My eyes filled up with tears of joy. "I missed you so much."

"Like I said, you should have come sooner! I missed you, too."

"No one told me anything. It's like I've been kept in the dark about everything."

"Well, everyone is okay as far as I know," she said, telling me about my older sisters and their families, my new nieces and nephews. She was still pretty close with some of our cousins. In fact, she was scheduled to spend the weekend with some of them in a few days. "And of course, Joan," she added.

My brows furrowed. *Joan? The awful thought of her had not been in my mind for some time now.*

I shook my head to clear it of the unpleasant thought of Joan, whom I hadn't contemplated in quite some time and was much happier because of her absence.

"It doesn't matter," I said to Michelle. "So much of my memory around those years, around that time, it's all mixed up. It doesn't matter."

We had only been talking for less than five minutes, but a tall woman had seen us and was approaching. Michelle saw her and said, "You better get going."

"But when will I see you again?" I asked hurriedly.

"I don't know. I'm going out to the cousins' this weekend."

I grinned mischievously. "No you're not," I said and winked at her.

I went to Cariter's House and checked her out that weekend. I was 18 after all, and a legal adult. I signed the necessary papers, and brought her back to Ruby's house where we talked for hours and hours. I told her how grown up she looked; she said that I was too tall and skinny, and that I needed to do something to tame my wild, curly hair. I showed her some of my art work and talked about my school, my friends. She had lots of questions about Ruby. I think she was partially curious and maybe just a little jealous, seeing that I had acquired a new family while she was still living in an institution.

What I remember most is that we both felt so free that weekend. We were so much older than when we last saw each other, and so we had so much more control over our lives -- or so we thought. I was going to go off into the world, into the Navy, soon. She wanted to get her driver's license, though it was still a few years off. We talked about how as we grew up, we weren't going to have to do what adults told us anymore.

The feeling of freedom was short-lived. When I was late bringing Michelle back to Cariter's House, police showed up at the house. Cariter's House had taken all my information, including the address, when I came to pick Michelle up, and they called the police when I didn't bring her back on time. They bundled her away in their squad car, as if I was going to kidnap her or something. Well, I admit, I did have a hard time letting go off my little sister so soon after being reunited. I would have kept her with me if I could.

But this time the parting wasn't so painful. I had seen her and talked to her, knew where she was, and how to get in touch with her. From that moment on, our bond was close and continued unbroken.

In my high school yearbook the year of my graduation, parents were asked to put in a family photo of their kids with a special parental message. I hadn't thought about that part of the yearbook at all until I saw what was waiting for me. There was a goofy photo of me smiling, and underneath was the message, "Thanks. From Ruby (Mom)."

My heart swelled. I felt like my life was actually going well. I felt like my life was going somewhere.

## Chapter Seven

My entry examination for the Navy was rather similar to the inspection I had received when I entered the Milford Assistance Program. I was deloused, examined orally, measured for height and weight. At one stage, a doctor did X-rays of my body for my military file and as we discussed my condition he asked me if I had even been in a car accident. Apparently, the photos of my bones had revealed several unset fractures that had calcified and a couple of minor spiral fractures that were not technically full breaks. I told him that no, I had never been in an accident and left it at that. I had survived the train wreck that was my abusive childhood and I didn't need to relive that with this total stranger. This was my new life now.

Recruits in the Navy are asked how they would like to specialize, what sort of job in the Navy they'd like to train for, and I decided to become a cryptologic technician. I thought that deciphering codes was really cool, thinking that my job would be glamorous and interesting, like some spy movie. In truth, the work consisted of differentiating between the pings of sonar that are sent out by submarines. I found myself out in California sitting in a chair with headphones on from 11 p.m. until 7 a.m., listening to pings. It was not glamorous. It was not Bondesque. It was downright boring.

I finally transferred to become a Captain's aid, which was much more to my liking. I was essentially the Girl Friday for one of the top brass of the Navy, traveling with him overseas and being his personal assistant. I did everything from organizing his paperwork to buying his wife's birthday presents.

About a year and a half before my time in the Navy was up, I had a casual relationship with an enlisted gentleman, and to my chagrin, became pregnant. It wasn't really my style, but there were a few times when I went with the flow of life, and this had been just such a time. The father was a sweet man, extraordinary in many ways, but we both knew that we were not destined to be together. Even so, he supported me through the pregnancy and beyond. That's how I found myself the proud mother of my daughter Nicole Marie (Niki), who was born at Pease Air Force Base in New Hampshire. I had eight months left in the Navy at the time of her delivery, a job in the tug boat office, and a pretty serious case of postpartum depression that Navy support and counseling helped me overcome.

Our family didn't stay only two members for very long. I attended a function for Naval officers and veterans and met a handsome and sweet man named Steven, who quickly became my husband and happily took on the role of being a dad to Niki as well, even if he wasn't her biological father.

At the time we met Steven was a nuclear submarine Engineer, but he was soon advanced to the rank of Commander, and eventually to that of Captain. Therefore, less than a decade after being a foster kid, bouncing around from place to place without a real home or any personal possessions, I found myself losing my New England accent (with lessons), hosting lunch parties, meeting important people and owning a small collection of glamorous evening gowns for formal events. I was the Captain's wife.

*The troubled girl who acted out. The tomboy who loved toads. Who would have thought?*

*

We had moved to Virginia Beach for Steven to take an assignment at the Norfolk Submarine Base. We decided to move out to the Kempsville area where the schools were known to be better. We moved into a subdivision called Brigadoon and purchased a home on Peggy Circle. This home had a lovely front porch area but it needed a little color. I purchased a couple of hanging baskets of potted hibiscus plants and much to my delight and surprise we attracted the cutest little creatures . . . hummingbirds. The hummingbirds loved to feed on the hibiscus flowers and I found myself buying more plants to attract more birds. Niki and I were amazed with the tiny birds that moved their wings so fast you couldn't even see them.

Steven and I wanted to have more children, but we faced significant obstacles. For one, a Naval officer, especially one who is under serious consideration for advancement to admiral, is often out at sea, and for *long* periods of time. His shortest cruises were for five to eight months, but 9 months and even 11 months wasn't rare. More importantly, I had experienced an ectopic pregnancy, a dangerous condition of which I was unaware. Using my artistic skills, I had a small business at the time as an interior designer that I absolutely loved, helping people make their environments beautiful. I was on a ladder at that time hanging a curtain when the ectopic pregnancy ruptured. I was taken to the hospital and doctors eventually had to remove one of my ovaries. My reproductive engines were only 50 percent viable, and I feared that I would not be able to conceive a second child to add to our family.

I suppose that's why my second daughter, Michaela Lynn -- who would always be known as Kaela among family and friends -- was always a miracle baby to me. Niki was six years old when Kaela was born, and where Niki had a pure Irish look about her with pale skin and red-gold hair, Kaela was more olive in complexion. She looked like she had been tanning while in the womb. So they were half sisters that didn't look alike at all, but both were an absolute joy to me.

I decided while pregnant with Kaela to decorate her nursery in the theme of hummingbirds. This was not an easy task as there was not a high demand for nursery items in a hummingbird pattern. I was lucky enough to have taught myself to sew and quickly found hummingbird fabric in the local fabric store. I set to work quickly making all of the crib bedding, comforters, pillows and bumper pads. I made cushions for the rocking chair, a hanging diaper holder and the window treatments. I loved my creation and quickly invited my friends to see my weeks of labor. My friends were not as impressed as I'd hoped, because the hummingbird colors were red and green. I tried to brighten the room up with some soft pinks and off-whites, but they complained that it looked more like a Christmas room than a nursery. Nonetheless, Kaela arrived and was completely happy in her room, created just for her.

Kaela learned of the beautiful birds as a toddler standing at the front glass door and watching in amazement as they whizzed by. Every once in a while one would come to the door for a private peek inside and she would laugh and bounce in complete joy over the close visitor.

One day Kaela wanted something in the garage which was off the hall near our kitchen. When I opened the door I saw what appeared to be a shriveled up balloon on the floor in front of my car. When I picked it up I realized it was one of the hummingbirds that most likely had become trapped in the garage and died from the heat. Kaela and I took the tiny creature out to our backyard behind the tool shed and gave the bird a proper burial.

*

It certainly was stressful being a mom with two small children and a husband who was rarely home to help. I had to be very structured and disciplined to keep up with everything, but I found that I thrived in structured environments.

My temperament had improved under Ruby's rules, and again in the military. But during the time I was out of the Navy and on my own in college, I didn't handle myself as well. I would sometimes have unexplained meltdowns or angry outbursts. These continued sporadically until I met and married Steven. I know it was due partially to the fact that I kept all my emotions -- and all my memories -- bottled up, until the cork just had to pop. I had suppressed a lot of memories, and those that were left were confused and distorted. My mind was a churning compost heap in many ways, attempting to break down and obliterate many of the experiences that had brought so much pain into my life. At different times I had even forgotten that Joan had survived the shooting, or that I had a boyfriend during high school, or that he was very angry with me because of something my strange friend had suggested to him. Indeed, my mind was like Swiss cheese, and whatever was roiling around in the subterranean regions was leaching up ever so slightly into my present world, agitating me in ways that I had difficulty understanding.

Focusing on my daughters and my family relieved that tension through pure, joyful activity and keeping busy.

I saw quite a few similar meltdowns and tantrums in my older daughter Niki, however. She could be a handful, and was eventually diagnosed with ADHD and put on medication. But her intense emotions were also a blessing.

When her sister was born, we lived in a neighborhood where all the other kids Niki had to play with were boys. One afternoon there was an intense rainstorm, a storm without thunder or lighting but that seemed to dump buckets from the sky. Niki had been playing outside in the yard with some of the neighborhood boys, and because I, too, liked the rain, I allowed her to stay out in the storm to play when she begged.

The downpour was such that there was no way the ground could soak up that much water. Within minutes there were huge puddles in the lawn. With Niki in the lead, all the kids started splashing in the puddles. Unafraid of getting dirty, they got down on the ground to roll in the mud, digging their hands into it and even throwing some of it around. Niki decided that the thing to do would be to show off her gymnastic skills to all her little boyfriends, so she got up to speed and did cartwheels and handsprings in the puddles. It made an impressive splash every time she landed.

Eventually the rain let up and the clouds started to clear. The kids were all soaked to the skin and breathless from their play, sitting sprawled in the muddy yard. To our mutual amazement, the largest rainbow I had ever seen spanned half of the sky, its colors crisp and clear. Niki's round little cheeks looked up at the sky, taking stock.

"Look!" she proclaimed. "God's done with his shower now, boys, and has painted the sky."

Her unbound joy and happiness was always infectious, and my heart ached with love when I thought about how special this pretty little girl was.

Due to of Steven's assignments, our little family did a lot of moving. After Virginia Beach, we spent time living in Washington State. Once again, after we settled in the girls and I decided to decorate the deck of our new home with the hibiscus flowers in hope that we would attract our little visitors as before in other locales. The house we rented was enormous with three levels of floor to ceiling glass windows. The home was obviously designed to offer a full view of the beautiful waters of Puget Sound and the mountains that framed it. We quickly noticed that the hummingbirds that came to eat were a little different in species, but were delighted in our offerings.

The girls and I were sitting in the kitchen one warm summer day enjoying lunch before they were to get into their little pool out on the deck. All of a sudden there was a bang at the window. I walked out on the deck and found the lifeless body of a hummingbird. The glass in the window was so clear it hadn't seen it. The tiny bird had broken its neck. The girls and I took it to the backyard and dug its final resting place. I remember a small twinge of uneasiness, but quickly put the thought out of my mind. There was some serious splashing to get into and get the somber mood out of our heads.

Of all the places that we moved to as a family, I think our house in Salem, Connecticut -- where we settled down for a little longer than usual -- was what the girls considered to be their childhood home. It was a large, gorgeous home more than 50 years old with an elegant, vintage feel to it. There was a large, sloping lawn and a pool in the backyard for the girls, which they were ecstatic about. While the girls were in school, I had a little in-home business called Michaela's Attic -- named after Kaela, of course -- that restored antique lamps.

This home had a nice big back deck with built-in seating. We settled into the home and once we were unpacked, bought hibiscus plants to hang. I was totally fascinated by the speed with which the birds could fly and I remember thinking it was too odd and way too coincidental that we had found two of the little creatures dead. They were on opposite sides of the country . . . they were two different species . . . but things do happen in three's . . . . I quickly abandoned the thought and went on to other tasks.

Fall was approaching and in New England you are lucky to squeeze a few warm days out of September. The evenings were getting cool and frost warnings were on the news in the forecast occasionally. The hibiscus leaves were starting to turn brown and the tiny visitors were becoming infrequent. Our fall clean up and pool winterization list was posted on the refrigerator. This was a great time of year where you could still enjoy a cup of coffee in the morning out on the sunny deck but the shadowed area had a noticeable temperature difference. Wrapped up in a big blanket and still in my pajamas I went out on the deck this one morning to enjoy my coffee and smell the fresh air. After I was settled in the sunniest spot on the built-in bench seat my eye caught a glimpse of something on the deck. I put down my coffee and walked over to it. Once again, one of the tiny creatures had succumbed to the afterlife. This one appeared to be unharmed and no broken neck. It was cold and clammy from the dew and its little feathers were wet. Its long sticky tongue was all the way out of its mouth. I didn't want Kaela or Niki to know the dead creature was there, so I quickly ran to the garage, snatched up some of my gardening tools and buried the little bird myself. I immediately took the hibiscus plants down that day and did not put new ones up the next year. When the girls asked about it, I told them I wanted to try a new type of flower to see what it would bring to us. I know this all sounds like an overreaction to coincidental circumstances, but I had convinced myself they were messengers of impending doom, and refused to invite them back. It suddenly bothered me greatly that I had used their image so generously in creating my baby's environment.

For a while it seemed that we had everything we needed and everything we wanted, but then parts of our idyllic family life started to unravel. Steven was wrapping up a 10-month cruise, which would end in Bangor, Washington. The girls and I were supposed to fly out to be with him for a while before he was deployed again, but they both managed to get extremely sick with what Pediatricians at the time were calling the Connecticut flu, a very dangerous strain for children. Because we couldn't meet up with him in Washington, Steven was sent out again for a six-month assignment, and it seemed ages before we set eyes on him, before he could hug the girls or me. All the contact that we had with Steven was on the phone or, when he was underwater on a submarine, through written messages the Navy called family-grams.

Meanwhile, back at home, it became increasingly obvious that the lovely old house we purchased was beautiful on the outside but rotting from within. It seemed the previous owners had fixed up the place beautifully with cosmetic changes, neglecting the really important things that needed to be fixed under the surface. One thing after another seemed to go wrong. The radiator clanked and wheezed. There was a mouse infestation. The roof was leaking badly.

After a weekend trip to visit my sister Michelle, we returned to the house to find that a pipe had burst and we were looking at a full-on flood. The carpet was a squelchy lake, and water ran down the banister from the upper level to the lower. Water from upstairs had weakened the ceiling of the main level and I found the dining room chandelier collapsed onto the dining room table. I had never seen such an utter mess.

It turned out the entire plumbing system needed to be replaced, a process that took months. At first, we went back to my sister's house. Then, as various parts of the house were completed one by one, we shifted our living quarters to whatever space happened to be available in our own home -- and not full of water or workmen.

Not everything that went wrong was catastrophic. For instance, the pool had a few hiccups that needed work. I had to learn to clean it and balance the chemicals in the water by myself. Then there was the lawn, which was absolutely gorgeous, sloping down from the street to flow around the house and down to a little wooded area. It made us feel like we were living on an estate rather than in a house. But then the neighbor boy wasn't able to mow it any longer, and the lawn began to grow shaggy and wild.

*Well, I am going to have to take matters into my own hands,* I decided. After Kaela's morning kindergarten class and while Niki was still in school, I went down to purchase a riding lawnmower from John Deere. Steven was from Wisconsin, the birthplace of John Deere, so it felt like the right choice. The trip actually turned out to be quite fun. We were showered with customer service and John Deere merchandise, like John Deere hats that Kaela thought were great, and I got talked into buying a large model with several gears.

We took home our beast of a lawnmower and Kaela would sit on my lap and help steer as we took on that large, imposing lawn and tamed it to our will. As she got bigger, we would strap pillows to her back and I'd let her use the gas pedal on the flat sections. Niki thought we were silly and wanted nothing to do our crazy mowing obsession.

The winters were long in that house, which I wound up wanting to demolish rather than fixing one more problem. In the end, it's not that I wasn't strong enough to handle being alone for long periods of time, taking care of two kids and being more independent. Instead, I felt frustration, because if I was really living this life on my own, why was I married?

When Steven finally came back to the family, walking through that door with the familiar, yet not so pleasant odor of diesel fuel about him, I thought, *Hmm, you look familiar, but who are you again?*

I loved Steven. He was an immensely good man, and I never regretted marrying him for a single second. But by the end of our 9 year relationship, we took out a calendar and added up that we had actually spent about four years living together. Those five years apart were just enough time for me to fall out of active love with my husband. He had been married twice before me -- though never for as long as our marriage had lasted -- and he would go on to marry twice more after me.

Perhaps I should have known. I'd repeatedly asked him to get a desk job instead of the active deployments he continued to seek.

"After this next cruise, I will," he always promised. "Just one more cruise out there."

The truth was that he loved being at sea. It was an addiction to being in the water that he couldn't shake if he tried, and it made him happy. If ending our marriage was going to make me happy (happier), then he would do nothing to stand in the way of me having the life that I wanted. It was one of the most amicable divorces I had ever heard of, for which I was immensely grateful.

I took custody of my daughters, both of whom still saw their fathers regularly. For vacations, Niki flew to New York to be with her dad and his huge, extroverted family. Kaela had regularly scheduled times with Steven, when he was in port, of course. In truth, I think those visits made both the girls feel very special in a way.

As for me, I met and married my second husband, Philip, with whom I ran a small government-consulting company. We lived in a large, quite lovely, custom home in South Riding, Virginia, which was located in Loudoun County, less than an hour's drive from Washington, D.C. Philip's daughter decided to live with her mother, but my two girls settled into a somewhat normal existence again, one where we didn't constantly move around the country and that I thought provided them with a more stable childhood.

Kaela especially seemed to thrive. When she was about seven years old, she joined the Loudoun County 4-H Club. She was at the age where a child's true personality begins to take shape and peek out around the edges, and it was obvious that Kaela's personality had a strong streak of determination.

The 4-H club is a group for young people that's especially popular in more rural areas. The Hs stand for head, heart, hands and health, and my little girl decided to master all of them. Over the course of a few months, she worked on her cooking and sewing skills. She'd ridden horses before, but she redoubled her efforts to become more skilled at it. And she was also very good at making crafts, and she loved that part of the experience.

The 4-H club has an annual fair, an event where all the kids come together for some friendly competition, followed by a fun celebration. Even though Kaela was relatively new to the organization, she won first place in more categories than any other child had in the past. She took the blue ribbons in baking, sewing, the essay competition and wreath design, and she placed second in barrel racing. In addition to the ribbons, she came away with $350 in prize money.

I was so proud of her. This was obviously a dedicated girl who wasn't going to settle for anything but the best and who had the perseverance to meet her lofty goals. And she did it all with a smile on her face and with kindness for others. Her good grades at school and her dedication to the swim team only further illustrated the fact that Kaela could set her mind on what she wanted and not give up until she had it in hand.

For instance, Kaela had once been very devoted to gymnastics and dancing ballet, tap and jazz. Then an accident on the trampoline fractured the humorous bone in her arm so severely that she required surgery to repair the bone with several metal pins. When she woke from surgery, she immediately attached herself to a teddy bear I'd bought her as a get well present which she named Cinnamon Bear. The painful fall and painful recovery took her out of dance for a while, and certainly gave her a healthy fear of the trampoline. But hugging that bear, she refused to just withdraw into herself and went right about doing the things she wanted to do, living her life. Cinnamon Bear therefore became her mascot, the comfort item that she turned to when she faced troubles or obstacles. A hug and a cuddle with Cinnamon Bear would lift her spirits and prepare her to get back out in the world again, to move on.

Happily, her injury did not take her out of the swimming scene for every long, and in fact, the doctor recommended it as part of her recovery to get her arm back into shape. Kaela was an avid swimmer from the time she had her first lesson at the age of two. The moment she hit the water, acting like a little human porpoise, was able to splash and glide through the water with natural talent and inclination. She felt a bond with the water, telling me, "Mom, I feel like a dolphin in the pool."

She joined the swim team at the earliest acceptable age and quickly began winning heats in her age group, specializing in the butterfly and breast strokes. Niki lost interest in swimming after a few years, but Kaela's love of the water never wavered. Over the years, she might have gone through a few stages where she got cocky and slacked off. When she started losing a few races, however, she'd always recommit herself to the sport. Both in winter (indoors) and summer (outdoors), I was Kaela's chauffeur to her passion for swimming. It was often hard to get up at the crack of dawn to drive her out to seven a.m. practices several times a week.

The normality of our family life compared with the chaos and negativity of my own childhood was a disparity that often struck me, sometimes as heartbreakingly wonderful and other times as quite surreal, that I had journeyed so far to such a different place than I had once been. I had travelled so long over so many obstacles that seemed as high as the

Rocky Mountains, and here I was in this safe, lovely house in a safe, lovely neighborhood. And my girls were safe, too.

I remember watching Kaela walk home from the bus stop after school with one of her close girlfriends, the two of them convulsed in a giggle fit about something. She was so carefree and happy, and my heart burst with pride. I remember waking up in the middle of the night to check on one of Niki's slumber parties. It may have been two a.m., but those goofy girls were painting toenails, braiding each other's hair, talking about boys and being absolutely normal. I was so glad she had teenage years that included such memories.

The three of us shared a very close bond, especially after the divorce from Steven. Since then, my husband Philip may have been in the family by marriage, but we were a family by blood. We took special note of holidays and birthdays, and my girls always gave me such thoughtful -- or sometimes silly, but equally wonderful -- presents.

One of our favorite things to do together, which we often started when there was something to celebrate or some tension that needed to be relieved, was food fights. I was and am an incredible neat freak who keeps my house white-glove clean, with everything in order and nothing unnecessary or out of place. But our food fights were the exception to the rule. They might start in the kitchen, but they'd range all over the house using whatever food was to hand as ammunition. The messier, the better. Desserts were always a favorite:

whipped cream, frosting, cupcakes and the like. Spaghetti is great, as is smashing butter onto another person's head or in her hair. Leftover holiday cranberry sauce was involved on at least one occasion. I'd later have to clean food off the floors, walls, tables, knick knacks and clothes, but food fights were a family tradition, a way of blowing off steam that brought us all closer together.

My girls were raised strict -- I put a lot of emphasis on doing well at school and not getting in trouble after it -- but with and equal emphasis on love and dignity, just as Ruby had raised men for those last couple of years of adolescence. The one thing that was never a part of their childhood, however, was mine. Steven had known the truth about my parents, as did Philip. The family members that I was in touch with, such as my sister Michelle, were under strict instructions that I did not want that particular episode of family history mentioned to my children, at least not until I thought they were ready. I told my girls that my parents had died in an accident when I was young and that I didn't know much more about it.

When Niki was 18, she was the type of girl who wanted full adulthood right away. Thanks to her strong independent streak, she left home relatively early to live life on her own terms. She leased a nearby apartment with a roommate, and we did see her quite often because, like a lot of 18-year-olds, laundry and buying groceries weren't her strong suit.

Nonetheless, I respected her for the mature woman she had become at 18, and decided it was time to tell her the truth about my past. It was a moment that I knew we were alone and that I hoped would be one of bonding and understanding between us. I laid out the facts that my mother was abusive, that there was a terrible incident where my father shot her and then himself, and that she survived and he died. I said that I had loved him. I said that while she was alive out there, she was not a person I wanted to waste any more of my time and energy on. She had already sapped so much out of me long ago and wasn't worth it. That, I told her, was how I eventually came to be in foster care, where I met the adoptive mother who Niki knew about.

"It's not something I talk about. It's not something I've ever talked about," I said. "But you're a woman now, and I thought it's something that you deserve to know."

"So Kaela doesn't?" she asked.

"No, and I don't think she should right now. I'll tell her, too, when the time is right."

## Chapter Eight

As Kaela grew up and entered high school, she continued to be both a high achiever at school and a very thoughtful, sweet girl to her friends and family. When her math class had a special study period or a big test, she loved to bake homemade chocolate chip cookies for the all of her fellow students, making an unpleasant task that much sweeter for everyone. During special weeks in the school year, she'd make a point to buy a dozen fresh roses. They had to be pink, of course, because that was her favorite. One rose was given to the bus driver, one was delivered to each one of her teachers, and she'd always save one flower just for me, her mother. It would always make me think of how small and adorable she'd been when we lived in the house surrounded by roses in Connecticut. It didn't seem like so long ago, and yet here she was, a young woman already.

Kaela loved the latest in all things, including music, clothes and other trends. In addition to founding a contracting company with my husband Philip, I worked in marketing for a local audio-visual firm where I was able to get Kaela a part-time job as a receptionist. She also babysat many nights and weekends for the neighbors' children. She loved to take her paycheck and go to the mall with her friends, shopping around for whatever cool thing they'd seen in the latest edition of their teen magazines. More often than not, she came home with the sillier, funkier type of clothes rather than high fashion. She preferred the ironic or witty T-shirts, her favorite being the fluffy white bear from the Snuggle Fabric Softener commercials.

She didn't spend all her money on frivolities, however. She also had a sizable savings account where she socked away money for the day she could buy a car. I had to admit, I was impressed by how fast and large she was able to make that account grow, though I shouldn't have been. If Kaela's mind was set on having a car, Kaela was going to make sure that wish came true.

She loved upbeat hip hop music and sang to every song on the radio whether in the car, the shower or at home. She was addicted to American Idol, never missing an episode and constantly talking about which contestants deserved to win. She also loved watching football, a passion that she picked up from her father. Like him, she was an avid Green Bay Packers fan. But she didn't have any problem balancing that love of sports with her more feminine and girly side, spending hours in front of the mirror working on her hair and make-up. Like most girls of that age, she wanted to look good while always worrying that she didn't look good enough.

Keeping her bathroom inhabitable and her room from attracting mice was always an issue. “Dishes belong in the kitchen not under your bed!” I would scold. “Kaela, this place is a pig sty! Clean it or you won’t be allowed out Friday night.” The usual large exaggerated huff would then be followed with the sarcastic “I KNOW.” I could never understand how a girl that kept all of her school books, assignments and papers so neat could live in such filth.

Kaela got excellent grades, all her teachers noting how focused and conscientious she was. She participated on the debate team, tutored other students, babysat for extra money and continued swimming. At the age of 14, her growing body made the latter more difficult. She was diagnosed with Osgood Schlatters Disease. The doctor explained that the pain in her legs was caused by her femur growing at a faster rate than her tibia, creating intense pressure and in some people's cases, even bone splinters. Swimming was supposed to help the condition, but at one swim meet it was so painful to Kaela that the moment she was out of the pool, I had to wrap warm towels around her legs while she winced and wept.

On top of that pain was the more emotional difficulty: Kaela had entered puberty early and developed a much larger chest than most of the girls her age. In swimming, such a development can not only slow down your speed, but can also cause embarrassment when you're self-conscious about your body.

So, at the age of 14, Kaela resigned from competitive swimming. However, she continued to help the swimming coach after school with the younger kids because she would always love the sport, taking the late bus home afterward because I was still at work at the audio-visual company. While I knew she would miss it, I was somewhat relieved to not have to be her crack-of-dawn driver.

Not everything was perfect with my budding teenage daughter. She was in her freshman year of high school and struggled with the adjustment. Like a lot of girls that age, she had her little disagreements with her friends. At home, she didn't get along with my husband Philip because she resented his presence in her life. He wasn't her father. He, in turn, didn't react very well, taking her negative attitude personally and arguing with her at a catty-schoolgirl level, as if there would be a winner and loser between a grown man and a 14-year-old girl. Even with me, she could be a little sarcastic and argumentative on occasion, although nothing out of line with normal teenage behavior. I would have to say the only really true annoyance that grated on my nerves was her constant correcting of everyone. She was like a damn encyclopedia of facts and she would not hesitate one moment to correct a person in a conversation even if she wasn't involved. It got so bad at one point I had to tell her that if she did it again she would be grounded the following Friday night. She couldn't help herself, I was on the phone less than five minutes later and walked by and corrected me on something I had just said. The weird part about it was that she was always right.

On the other hand, I did see a great deal of the positive in Kaela, her talents and her potential. I was struck in particular by the amazing young woman my daughter was becoming during a school assignment she had that year, which required my help. I don't remember what class the assignment was for, but the idea was to study the effect of various forces, events or other stimuli on humans; what changed in their behavior, in their future destinations or in their personality. Kaela's idea was to research homelessness. Are there certain events or personality traits that lead to someone being homeless, or lead them to stay that way?

I thought it was an interesting idea, certainly, but there was some question about how she would be able to carry out this research. We planned for a while and came up with the idea of driving over to nearby Washington, D.C. I would go with Kaela to try to speak to any homeless people that we encountered, which would be quite a few in D.C., and Philip would stay in the nearby car, just in case something went wrong and we needed him to intercede or wanted to make a quick getaway.

Many of the people we approached wouldn't speak to us, and I didn't blame them. We were two relatively privileged white women who wanted to know about all the things they'd experienced in life, and that's personal business -- and negative memories at that -- something I understood. Some were strung out, drunk or high. However, with the incentive of a $5 bill and a warm blanket -- we'd taken a stack to give away, thinking blankets would be the most useful commodity on a cold night -- some of the people we met along the street and alleys began to tell us how it was that they came from where they used to be to that particular cardboard box or vent grate.

Both of us were simply amazed at some of the stories we heard. Doctors, a dentist, a man with a Ph.D., and business professionals. The backgrounds of the people we talked to were varied and surprising, often more privileged than we would have imagined. All did have stories of tragedies, real or imagined, including the death of a family member, being left by a spouse, losing a job, or paranoid ideas about someone or something being after them. We sat on the ground cross-legged, and Kaela wrote down their stories in a lined, spiral notebook.

What impressed this project of Kaela's so firmly in my memory was reading the thoughtful and surprising report she put together about the stories and experiences we'd gathered. All of these people had come from places where lots of other people did, too. Lots of other American people had the same sort of education, home environment or career. Plus, many other people in the population have suffered the same tragedies of death, divorce or even mental illness. And yet, only a very small percentage of people took those experiences and became homeless long-term as a result.

Granted, hardship could land you on the streets, she concluded, but it was attitude that kept you there. She thought that resigning yourself to that life and not actively seeking to improve it showed that these men and women were making a choice. Working and living and loving and engaging the real world took a lot of hard work. It meant having to fight and care and be passionate about something. Kaela concluded that homelessness was basically a *choice* to withdraw from the battle of life because the battle at some point had become too difficult to fight any longer.

Her understanding of human nature and of the nature of life itself astounded me at the time, coming from a girl who wasn't even old enough to qualify for a learner's permit to drive the car she was saving up for.

*

In the neighborhood where we built our house, the nearest grocery store was the Food Lion and I was as regular a shopper at that supermarket as most other people in the area. I was certainly in the store enough that I got to know some of the employees, and some of them came to remember me, if not my name then certainly my face. It was the kind of neighborhood where people were friendly like that, nodding and smiling at one another or making casual conversation.

I always had to shake my head and laugh at one particular Food Lion employee, however. He was a young man named David, according to his name tag, and he was a prankster. He was average height and lean, the kind of kid that even at the age of 19 might grow a few more inches. His slender face always seemed to be grinning in a way that was both mischievous and goofy.

Numerous times when I'd finished my shopping and got into line to wait for a cashier, I'd find silly things in my cart that I certainly hadn't put there: cigars, Depends adult undergarments, and other potentially embarrassing items. *What?* I'd think to myself, staring down at the unknown item in my hand. Then I'd snap my head up and look around the store to see who might be watching. And there would be David, his head peeking out from around the corner of a nearby aisle, trying to hide his giggles behind his hand, his shaking shoulders giving him away.

Once I figured out his game, I kept an eye out for that prankster, but he was sneakier than I would have thought. Even when I saw him elsewhere -- such as with a mask, gloves and a spray bottle of disinfectant cleaning the butcher's room, safely separated from the store by glass -- he'd enlist other friends to keep up the game. I'd find fried pork rinds or some other crazy thing in my cart only moments later.

"Have to keep you happy," he told me later when I asked about how he'd pulled that one off. He was working as cashier that day, scanning the things that I did want to buy. "You have to keep the customer happy," he explained, grinning at me.

Granted, this kid David and I didn't have a real relationship. He was just a silly young man who worked at a store where I often went. We did have a few conversations, however.

For instance, one evening when I was picking up a few last-minute things for dinner, I walked in to find that David suddenly had a Mohawk haircut. His brown hair was still as long as it ever had been in one long strip along the center of the top, but the sides of his head were completely shaved. It's a style that managed to look both bad and rebellious, as well as downright silly.

"Well, what on earth?" I asked him. "What happened?" I gestured at his head.

"What? This?" he said, rubbing a hand along the hair he still had left. "This is what happens when the old man gets drunk."

"No!" I exhaled dramatically, immediately reacting with disbelief.

"I'm afraid so," he replied, nodding solemnly. He managed to almost completely block his grin, the serious expression broken by the slightest turning up of the edges of his mouth.

I had to shake my head at the prank and let it go.

Another time a month or so later, I saw that he was scanning groceries awkwardly, hampered by a cast on his hand surrounding his thumb. He made up an obviously concocted and crazy tale about how he'd been injured. It was too wild to be believed, something about skydiving or a motorcycle or stopping a crime being committed. I don't remember. He had actually hurt himself doing something much more mundane: playing basketball with his buddies. But the kid had imagination. If life wasn't that interesting, I guess he thought he had to make it interesting all by himself, however he could manage it. It was a little endearing I thought.

For a while, that's the only part David played in my life; he was cast in the role of the goofy guy I sometimes ran into at the store. It was only later, much later, that I realized the very moment when he'd auditioned to play a much larger, very consequential role in the story of my family, transforming from a kid who worked at the store into a catalyst that changed all of our lives forever.

The initial incident occurred on a day which up until that point had unfolded just likc it had dozens of times before.

Since the time that Niki moved out of the house, I had made it a point to spend quality time with Kaela, who had been left as the only child to echo around in an otherwise empty house. One of the things that became our ritual was to get our nails done together about every other week. It was something that I had done for a long time in order to feel professional and polished on the job.

But at 14, Kaela was old enough to appreciate the glamour of having her nails done professionally and mature enough to take decent care of the final result.

As we left that evening, Kaela said, "I'd like to bring cookies in for math class tomorrow."

"Now?" I asked, looking at my watch. "You'll never have time. It's already pretty late."

"No, we can just run in and get one of those pre-made tubes of dough, Mom. It will only take five minutes, and they still taste pretty good in the end. Please?"

And that's how we came to be waiting in line at Food Lion with cookie dough, a gallon of milk and a few other staples that we needed back at home. Waiting in David's line, as it turned out.

He smiled at me, his typical lopsided grin, and said hello. He went on to bandy about some of his standard repartee, saying something like, "Well, now. Let's see what you have in your cart this time, shall we?"

I stood to his right, sliding the items toward him and the scanner. Kaela took up position on his left where she was being considerate, taking over the bagging of our groceries herself. As well as looking at what was in my cart, it was obvious that David was also looking at who I'd brought with me. He was being surreptitious about it, glancing up at her from under his eyelashes as he scanned the groceries, and at that moment I saw my daughter in a completely different way. I saw her the way that this 19-year-old must see her, as a pretty and curvy girl who looked much older than 14 years thanks to her developed chest. She probably could have been mistaken for 19 pretty easily.

Not that the two did any overt flirting. It seemed to me that David was just being himself.

"So where do you go to school?" he asked her.

She looked up and met his eye, perhaps the first time she'd actually been paying attention.

"Broad Run High School," she said. "Freshman." She intentionally said the word with a sense of irony, as if she was sick and tired of being teased for being on the bottom of the ladder.

"Oh, I already graduated from there," said David, probably trying to impress her. "I'm in college over at ITT Tech now." But he wasn't going to get off that easily with Kaela.

"Well la-di-da," Kaela replied, rolling her eyes.

For a moment he looked shocked, and he looked back at me to see if this girl was for real. I just gave his own smirk back to him. Then he burst out with a short laugh and I could see them make eye contact again, firm contact, meaningful. I watched the line between their eyes as I signed the bill for the groceries.

David took the last bag and handed it to Kaela. "You know the Spartan head that's right inside the school foyer?" he asked.

"Yeah."

"Don't you get caught standing on it," he said, as if he was imparting a mysterious and dangerous secret.

"Why?" she asked, taking the bait.

"Because the seniors have a right to make you clean it with a toothbrush if they catch you. The teachers don't even care. They'll let them do it and leave you there for hours with just a tiny little brush."

She tilted her head skeptically. "No way."

Now it was time for me to roll my eyes. That was classic David, always cracking some kind of joke.

As we walked back to the car, Kaela asked me what I thought, saying, "Do you really think that if a senior finds me on that big circle, I'll have to scrub the whole thing?"

"I don't know. I don't go to school there," I replied. "But I guess so."

She shook her head. "Well, I'm not going to get anywhere near that, then."

I laughed. We went home and the house soon filled with the aroma of chocolate chip cookies. Before Kaela left for school the next morning, I snuck one of the little delights for myself as I headed off to work.

She was right. The pre-made ones were still pretty good.

## Chapter Nine

The first time that Kaela met David in the Food Lion took place in December. As strange and almost ominous as it was, the incident had not made a huge impression on me. Perhaps David acted slightly different toward me when I next saw him in the store, maybe a little nicer, even a little bit sucking up. I just thought, *He thinks my daughter's cute.*

After all, she was a 14-year-old girl, and he was a 19-year-old man. A six-year difference might not be much between grown-ups of middle age, but that was an ocean apart in maturity and approachability at Kaela's age. There was no way it could happen, so I didn't give things a second thought.

And if there was some way it could happen, there was no way that I as her mother was going to let it. Or so I thought. Teenagers, after all, have minds of their own.

It was several months later, in March or April, that I got a phone call from the manager of the Food Lion. I was very involved in our little town and so was on friendly terms with most of the local businesspeople, including the grocery manager. We knew each other well enough that while it didn't happen often, I didn't think it too unusual that he was taking the time to call me that afternoon.

"What can I help you with?" I asked.

He cleared his throat. "Well, Lorijane, it's not my business, and I know that," he said. "But I've been thinking about it a lot and I wanted to tell you. Kaela is a great kid and she's really sweet and everything. We love her! But she's only fourteen, and if she were my daughter, I would want someone to let me know."

"Let me know what?" I asked, wondering what on earth she had done that he would be saying this on the phone. My heart was beating faster, imagining the possibilities. "Did she do something wrong?"

"No, no," he said. "Nothing like that."

I waited a moment before urging him on. "Go on."

"It's David, David Kompo. One of our cashiers."

"Yeah, the Mohawk kid. I know him."

"Right. Well, instead of going straight home after school, Kaela's been coming around here to hang out with David. I think they're dating."

My mind was suddenly flooded with pictures that were difficult to put together. How could Kaela have gotten together with David? Why would she? He was way too old, and she knew how I felt about that kind of thing. There was no indication that she was even interested in a boy . . . or in this case, a man. "Over my dead body," I said, my voice high-pitched and upset.

"He's 19 years old, and like I said, she's fourteen," the manager continued. "I thought you needed to know."

"Yes, I did. Thanks so much for keeping an eye out for Kaela."

"Anytime," he said.

I got the call on my mobile phone at work, and the first thing I did when I got home was to sit Kaela down in the living room for a little chat. I had taken a lot of deep breaths and gone over what I wanted to say in my head so I wouldn't go overboard, wouldn't freak out about what might turn out to be nothing.

"Kaela," I said. "I've been hearing a few things about you lately, and I want to know. What's going on?"

She was perched on the couch, each hand on the opposite elbow, hugging herself.

"What's going on with what?" she asked innocently.

"What's going on with you and David? This David Kemps?"

She didn't want to directly meet my eyes, but I waited, letting her squirm. I realized that her ears were flushed bright red.

"Yeah, we kind of like each other, Mom," she finally said.

"Well, that's very nice that you kind of like each other," I replied. "But you are not going to date David Kemps. For one, you're fourteen and not old enough to date. Plus, even if you could, he's twenty years old!"

"So what? Age doesn't matter," she protested quickly as though she'd rehearsed that line a hundred times.

"It does when you're only fourteen," I corrected. "It does." My voice was getting louder than I'd meant it to be, but I was still relatively calm. I was trying to be firm, yet reasonable, the way Rubynie was with me when I was a turbulent teenager.

"Now, I'm not saying that there's anything wrong with David, but a romantic relationship with him is not right. It's not going to happen. You just need to break it off. Tell him your parents won't let you date, not at all, and blame it all on me if you want to, but that's a relationship that you need to stop. Now."

She was still looking down at her knees.

"Kaela?"

It took her a few more moments to look up and meet my eyes. She looked disappointed, maybe a little angry. Then she took a deep breath and let it out.

"All right, Mom," she said. "I'll break it off with David."

I sat beside her and put my arm around her shoulders, and kissed her hair. "Besides," I whispered in her ear, "you're my baby. You're not going to date until you're fifty anyway."

We both laughed a little, but neither one of us was happy.

*

Everybody seemed to know what was going on but me. Everyone but me had seen that Kaela and David were still dating, were definitely a couple. When Kaela said she was going out with friends, she would meet up with David instead. They went to parks after school, or over to David's house. They went to the mall and to the movies. They didn't get called out about their relationship until David was brazen enough to pick up Kaela after school in his pick-up truck, driving right up to the curb where his former teachers, classmates and their parents could easily recognize him.

It was June when another mom called my cell phone with more bad news about David Kemps and my daughter, and Kaela was still just 14, still far too young to be getting involved with an older man who was in college and could easily take advantage of her. I wondered if he already was taking advantage of her age. After all, she'd never lied to me like this before, and a convincing older man might be the explanation for that behavior.

"But I like that he's in college, Mom," she said when I angrily confronted her about the continuing relationship. "He's not like the stupid boys in my class. And he loves me."

"Loves you? He loves you?"

"Yeah, and I love him, too," she said, her hands on her hips.

"Well, love him from afar then, Kaela," I replied, "because you're not going to see him anytime soon."

She threw her arms up in the air as if I was the one being impossible.

"You don't understand, Kaela," I said. "A relationship like this is actually illegal, and there's a good reason for that. Such an older guy can really take advantage of you, hurt you. It's for your own protection that society shields young girls from older men, because girls are easy prey for them, it's not because I don't want you to have a boyfriend."

She looked a little more sheepish now, so I went on.

"But you know what really disappoints me? You lied to me about ending it. I thought I could trust your honesty."

"Oh, Mom," she said, and she started to cry. I took her in my arms. "It just sucks. I finally meet a guy that I like, and I can't be with him. Why does it have to suck?"

"Shh." I brushed her hair back from her forehead. "I know, it hurts. But it really is best this way. And besides, school is out very soon and we'll have a great summer -- away from David, right?"

She looked at me with teary eyes and nodded.

"Good. We're going to have a great summer."

We did have a beautiful summer. Our family was lucky enough to have a boat that we often took out from a local marina. Most weekends you could find us sunbathing on the upper deck, where Kayla would tease me about how much tanner she could get than me. Her friends -- the friends I knew and who were of her own age -- were always welcome to come, and regularly did. And because Kaela was the only kid in the house, her friends often slept over throughout the summer.

"Mom, I'm so over David," Kaela had said when I asked about how she was feeling. I wanted to let her know that it was okay to be sad about the situation, even if it was a necessary sadness. I understood puppy love, and knew that it was really wonderful when it happened, and really painful when the breakup came. I was a kid too, at one time. I wanted her to know that I understood how she was feeling. Even if she said she was over a David, I knew there would be lingering sadness for a while, until it was replaced by something else.

I started to believe her, however, when one afternoon after she'd had a group of friends over, I found a notebook on the kitchen table. From what I could tell, it was a slambook all about David, a place where the girls had put every negative thing they could think of about Kaela's now ex-boyfriend. David is scrawny. David has funny hair. They'd written silly and awkward poetry making fun of David. There were words and drawings as well as photos cut out from various places. I thought the whole thing was quite funny, but part of me was also very proud. This was obviously something cathartic that Kaela had to do in order to get over her first big crush, and it meant she was moving on.

I really believed it, which made me think that at least to a certain degree, Kaela believed it, too. Or maybe not, maybe the whole summer was an act.

Come fall when school started up again, I got a call from a family friend that Kaela was just that afternoon at the movies with David Kemps, and I got angry, of course. Because my daughter was still lying to me. Because this boy was luring her to do things she wasn't supposed to do, and lie to me, luring her into dangerous waters. That no one else seemed to be willing to say or do anything about it.

Before Kaela got home from her little liaison, I decided that I needed to enlist another mother's help. I called David's step-mother, Marion, his biological mother having left him and his father on their own a long time ago.

"Hello?"

"Yes, hello. This is Lorijane, Kaela's mother. Is this Marion?"

Her voice was a little surprised but not unfriendly. Cautious, just like my own.

"Yeah, that's me," she said. "How can I help you?"

"Well, like I said, I'm Kaela's mom. I don't know if you know this or not, but my daughter is only fourteen years old. Now, I know she's been hanging around with David -- dating David -- and I thought maybe we could help each other."

"What do you mean?" She sounded confused by the notion of either of us needing help.

"Well, I don't really approve," I clarified, surprised that it wasn't obvious to her. "I think that -- "

"And what exactly is wrong with my son?" she asked, getting quite defensive very quickly.

"Nothing. I didn't say anything was wrong with David," I said, baffled by her reaction, trying to calm her down so we could talk about this. "It's just that she's fourteen and he's nineteen, and by any standards, that's really inappropriate."

She was silent for a moment, so I continued, "I was hoping that we could come to a mutual understanding here and have some support on both sides, because I don't want this to continue. It's just a dangerous situation for a young girl to be in."

"I hate to burst your bubble, Lorijane, but for one, David is nineteen years old. It's not like he's a kid that we can just order around and tell what to do," she said. "And he likes Kaela. Heck, we all like Kaela. She makes him happy."

She makes him happy? This wasn't going very well at all. This woman seemed to be missing the important parts of this conversation. "With all due respect," I continued, "there is more at stake here than either of their puppy love feelings. He is an adult, as you say, and that means that if he has any kind of physical relationship with my daughter at fourteen . . ."

"What?"

"Well, it's statutory rape, because he's an adult and she's only fourteen."

"Are you accusing my son of raping her?!"

This conversation was not going as I had planned and obviously wasn't going to end with "mutual understanding." In fact, I felt like I had stirred a hornet's nest with a stick and was going to feel the sting of it soon enough.

"No, no, I'm not saying that. I'm saying the law says that," I corrected. "It's an unfortunate situation all around, and I hoped we could understand each other. But I'm sorry. I'm sorry I called."

I hung up the phone and immediately covered my mouth with my hand, upset to the point of being near tears because I was trying, I was trying so hard. I was trying to do the right thing. I had nothing against David in an objective sense. He was goofy, sure, but he was at least in school, even if it was a tech school that took even mediocre students. His family was very different from our own, slightly lower on the social totem pole perhaps, but I had no bias against where people came from. My own background had taught me a great deal about such judgments.

And yet, this situation with my daughter in "love" with this young man was not tenable. She was acting in ways that she'd never done before, lying and sneaking around, perhaps being emotionally manipulated. I knew I was right in putting an end to it . . . again.

When she walked back into the house, fresh from her movie date, I told her that I knew where she had been.

"Yeah, so I've been seeing him, okay?" she said, defensive and defiant.

"And how did that start again?" I asked. She didn't answer, so I continued, "Is he pressuring you to date him again?"

Again, she was silent, her lips pursed tightly. I was still very upset, but I tried to keep my voice level and authoritative. "If that's the way it's going to be, with you lying to me and sneaking around and breaking the rules," I said, "then the deal is off." I was talking about her upcoming 15th birthday party a few weeks away in October, for which we'd already started making big plans. "The whole party, the limo for your friends, everything. It's off."

"Mom!" she yelled. "You can't do that!"

"And you can't have an illegal relationship with a nineteen-year-old man and lie about it to your parents!" I retorted quickly. "That's the action. Canceling the party is the consequence."

"You are impossible!" she shouted, turning to stomp up the stairs in high teenage style. Her face was bright red and already damp from tears about to explode.

Now, Niki had some behavioral issues as she was growing up, and I had handled those problems as they arose. But this behavior from Kaela seemed different. She was never a disobedient child -- opinionated about what she wanted, perhaps, but never destructively willful. She was a fantastic student, a big help around the house. We had a close and loving relationship. But this situation had gone too far. There was no way that I, as a conscientious mother, could allow my young teen to date a man six years her senior at that tender age. It would be irresponsible, to the point of child abuse, to allow such a relationship. I could just see Oprah or Jerry Springer browbeating a trailer park mother for not having any better sense than to allow her daughter to date a man. "What were you thinking?! Didn't it occur to you that your fourteen-year-old child was too young to be in a romantic relationship with a young man in college?! How can you pretend to be shocked that she's pregnant?! *Oh god*, I thought. *Pregnant*. No, my little Kaela needed, and deserved a better mother than that. Being unpopular with a fourteen-year-old wasn't as important as being the mother I knew my fourteen-year-old needed.

I knew that I had to restrict her in order to keep her safe from this young man, an adult with obviously really bad judgment. She was grounded for starters, and put on a short leash -- I told her that she needed to call me from the home phone as soon as she got home from school every day. The neighbors agreed to look out for strange cars or trucks in the driveway. She was allowed to go out of the house for school, extracurricular activities, or with supervision.

Kaela was not happy with the situation, of course, but life did go on. Eventually we agreed that she could have friends over to the house again, and that she could go out as long as we knew where she was, who with, and we drove her to and from. And she still was allowed to help out with the younger kids' swim team practices, taking the late school bus home.

One evening that fall when she arrived home, she had with her a ring, explaining that the sparkle of it in the sand by the bus stop had caught her eye. Knowing I was a gemologist, she let me take a look.

"It's real, looks like," I said.

"You can tell just by looking?" she asked.

"It's a small, little diamond, but it is a diamond."

"Wow, huh," she said, looking again at her find.

She looked a little bit happy for the first time in a while. Plus, we were having a conversation that wasn't angry. It seemed like a step in the right direction, and so I let her keep the found ring. Always a stickler for the rules, I told her that we should file a police report. If the ring wasn't claimed, it was legally hers. It seemed like a minor thing, but she smiled. I loved to see her smile.

*

With this uneasy truce, we moved as a family through the fall that Kaela turned 15. When Christmas came around it seemed like Kaela had turned another leaf. She was acting more like herself again, affectionate and joking with me, talking a lot on the phone with her friends and otherwise being a normal girl of that age.

I had been able to take a deep breath and relax my stressful vigil a bit. It also helped everyone's attitude that the holiday season was approaching, meaning a big Christmas celebration at home and then Christmas break from school. For as long as we'd been divorced, Steven and I had arranged that Kaela would spend the actual Christmas holiday with one parent and share the rest of her school break with the other parent, and then do the reverse the next year.

Maybe it was the Christmas spirit at work on my emotions, but a day or two before Christmas, Kaela casually mentioned to me that she'd heard from David.

"No, we haven't been seeing each other. We just talked very briefly," she assured me, holding up her hand to fend off my possible reaction. "It's actually that he feels bad about what he did, about getting me in trouble with you and everything."

My thoughts all deserted me for a moment as I tried to wrap my mind around this complete reversal. "And what does he want to do about it?" I asked cautiously.

"He wants to come over to the house and say sorry to you, if that's okay," she said. "So that he can apologize."

I was conflicted. Having David come over seemed like an overwhelmingly bad idea, but then again, who was I to tell him that he couldn't make amends for something he thought was wrong? Obviously, it was a silly gesture, a little immature even. However, it was the holiday season, so I told Kaela that he could drop by.

That's how he came to stand outside my door on that cold winter night. In one hand he carried a bouquet of flowers, the kind you pick up get at a grocery store, and in the other he held a bottle of perfume. We met at the front door and he came no further inside the house, Kaela making a point to stay down the hallway a little, where she could see but not be in the way.

"Thanks for letting me come," he said, coughing a little to clear his throat. "I just wanted to say sorry. I really didn't mean to cause so much trouble."

I nodded and reached out to accept the gifts from his hands.

"Thanks," I said, softly. I was unsure of what to do in this strange situation. Finally, I decided that it would be best to keep it short and simple. "Merry Christmas, David."

"Merry Christmas," he repeated.

I closed the door and shot a look at Kaela behind me. She gave me a kind of half smile and a shrug.

*

After Christmas, I didn't see Kaela for more than a week while she spent her vacation with her dad, at his house in Wisconsin. His parents, Kaela's grandparents, still lived up there, so it was always a big, warm family event when she traveled up north with him. The day after she left, perhaps already missing her around the house, my mood was instantly cheered when I opened a kitchen cabinet and something small and soft fell out. I caught the object in my hand and saw it was a stuffed monkey, a Beanie Baby. He was wearing a hat on which Kaela had written “Mr. Omish Monkey Hat” in goofy print.

I had to smile. It was a tradition of sorts that Kaela had made up a few years before, leaving me a little something in a very unexpected place when she went out of town without me. Her way of saying that she wasn't really gone, that she was thinking of me. On another occasion, I reached into my dresser drawer for a pair of pantyhose, which didn't seem to want to come out. Looking closer, I saw that the silly girl had put an avocado in the foot of the hose, knowing I'd need to grab them to dress for work.

Even if I did miss her, I know Kaela had a great time on trips up to visit her dad and his family. To make things even better, Steven was the person with whom Kaela shared her obsession for football, and he'd scored them tickets for a game at Lambeau Field while she was there.

They were both diehard Green Bay Packers fans. I think Steven passed that along as his genetic contribution to Kaela, because I sure didn't understand the appeal. It was freezing in December, and I would rather be indoors than frozen to a hard bench trying to see a football game through the frost of my own breath.

However, there was no stopping Kaela. Like so many Green Bay fans, she was deeply enamored of quarterback Brett Favre and one of her biggest wishes was for his autograph. Kaela usually was up north with her dad for their training camps every year, when she'd wait outside the chain link fence as the players walked back from the field, hoping and praying he'd stop and say hello. He never had. She came early to the games and stayed late, hoping for the same, but it just never happened.

For Christmas that year, I'd given both Steven and Kaela the gift of battery-powered seat warmers to keep them from shivering in the cold as they watched the game. Both were emblazoned with the Green Bay team logo, of course. That wasn't the only thing decked out for the team, however. Kaela also had an oversized Favre jersey that would fit over her coat, and she painted his number -- #4 -- on her face for the live games. She must have been memorable, I'll say that.

On the way out, Steven bought her a new jersey to take home because the one she wore to school was growing faded, and they headed out. This time, however, they just got lucky. They walked by a hallway where Brett Favre himself was being interviewed by a handful of reporters with still and video cameras. Star struck, Kaela stopped to watch. Maybe it was the face paint or the jersey, but something about her caught her idol's eye.

"Hey," he said. "I've seen you at the fence before. You come all the time, right?"

Her eyes grew wide and her jaw dropped, but she managed a nod through her excitement.

He put his hand up to put the reporters on hold for a moment. She quickly handed over her jersey and he scribbled his autograph on it with a marker.

"Thanks for all your support over the years," he said, and then turned back to his interviews.

"That-Was-Amazing," she said to her dad, who later told me that she basically floated all the way back home and would talk about nothing else for the remainder of the visit. I saw that he wasn't exaggerating when he arrived back at our house with Kaela about 10 o'clock in the evening on the last day of her winter break. She was just exploding with the excitement of her encounter.

"Mom! He signed it! He signed it!" she shouted, bouncing a little in her ecstasy. She immediately threw down her suitcase and started rooting around to find the jersey, which she then held up for me like it was the greatest trophy in the world.

I beamed brightly, happy to see my daughter so overjoyed. "That's so awesome!" I said. "I can't believe it finally happened. Did you guys get a picture of him?"

"We were a little too shocked and excited," admitted Steven sheepishly. "I even had my cell phone, but . . . ."

Kaela continued rooting around in her bag, coming up for air to show me her new Green Bay socks and banners and other souvenirs, which were spilling all over the floor. She was bouncing off the walls, taut as a bowstring.

"I know, Honey. It's great," I said, coming over to put my arm around her shoulder. I met Steven's eye and we both shook our heads, still smiling. "It's late for tonight, though. You have school in the morning. Pick up your stuff, get ready to go to bed, and we'll celebrate tomorrow, okay? It's fine."

She still had the gleam of excitement in her eyes, but she nodded and headed upstairs with her hastily re-zipped suitcase.

I said goodnight to Steven, saw him out, and headed off to bed myself.

## Chapter Ten

The next morning, January 3rd, began like any other workday for me or any other school day for Kaela, though perhaps she was a little more tired and sluggish due to her late arrival from her Christmas vacation with Steven. Philip had already left for the city so I was alone, straightening up the kitchen and drinking my morning coffee as I usually do. Philip and I jointly ran a contracting company and worked on site in the city. I also had a position in marketing that was my true day job, to which I commuted a short distance every day.

Kaela and I had a morning routine. Rather, I had a routine that I used to make sure she made it to the bus on time because I couldn't drive her in the car every day. The routine began with me knocking loudly on her door, perhaps a few times, until I heard her shout, "I'm up, mother!" The *mother* dripped with teenage tone.

"I'm making your breakfast, so hurry up."

"Okay!"

Recently, Kaela had begun dragging her feet until later and later, sometimes running out the door with no breakfast and her coat half on. I found being proactive was very helpful in sending a fully dressed and prepared freshman to high school.

She ran in for breakfast and ran back upstairs.

"You have ten minutes," I called after her. "And you didn't drink your orange juice."

She trotted back in with her school bag, books and outerwear, grabbed the juice and drank.

"Did you brush your teeth?" I asked, thinking about how much I hated the combination of orange juice and toothpaste.

As she drank, she nodded and grimaced. I had to laugh.

I looked at the time and realized I had to go. I hugged her, then did the typical mom thing I did every morning. "I'm leaving now," I said. "I love you."

"I love you!" she said, as I turned to go.

"I love you," I tossed back over my shoulder.

As I entered the garage, I heard her yell one last time, "I love you!"

I rolled my eyes, but was actually always tickled by this little game of trying to be the last one to say, "I love you." Sometimes I would get on my cell phone and it would continue all the way to work, seeing who could outlast the other in the game. This time, I yelled back, "I love you!" Then I shut the door, making sure I got the last word out.

It was Monday. For me, it was a very normal Monday at work for the most part, busy but not unpleasant. For Kaela, it was most unusual, but I had no idea of that at the time. I knew she'd gotten on the bus and gone to school, and thought no more of it. People talk about women's intuition -- or even the more powerful mother's intuition -- but if I've ever experienced the phenomenon, it wasn't on that unseasonably warm January day. I had no supernatural feelings or vibes. I had only my regular, old eyes and my regular ears, and all my normal senses. And so to relate how things unfolded for us, I think I must begin with the day as I experienced it.

I worked until 5:00 or 5:30 in the evening on most days, but Philip got home from the city a little earlier, about 4 in the afternoon. It was about 4:15, the approximate amount of time it would have taken him to park the car, come inside the house and go into his office, where he sorted through the mail and dealt with other small business. From the office, he'd usually cut through the kitchen to the door to the backyard deck. He still smoked cigarettes, even if I wouldn't allow him to smoke anywhere inside the home, being as neat as I was and cringing at my childhood memories of cigarette-smokey, stuffy houses.

It was then that I got a phone call, looking down to see it was Philip's cell phone. He didn't even give me time to finish the word hello before he started blurting, obviously upset.

"Get home, Lorijane. Get home now!"

"What's going on?" I asked, unsure whether to be angry or frightened at his tone. The latter was certainly taking control, my heart climbing further up my throat.

"Just get home, now!"

I heard the noise of another voice nearby his receiver, as if he was talking into two phones at the same time. He was beginning to answer the other voice when he hung up and the line went dead.

I stared at the face of the phone for only a moment, but I couldn't just not know what was going on to make my husband so frantic. I flipped open the phone and dialed him back.

"Philip, tell me."

"The kids. Kaela," he said. His voice broke. "Just come."

The line went dead again, and this time, I grabbed up my keys and purse and hurried toward the door. I shouted something over my shoulder to my coworkers about a family emergency. Frankly, I don't remember what it was I said. I was in full-on mother bear mode, running full speed toward a cub in danger.

But how was she in danger? I needed to know, so I dialed one more time as I opened the driver's door of my car, the phone wedged between my shoulder and ear.

"I'm on my way. Just tell me," I said when Philip answered. I heard the sound of another voice again, a voice over a phone line. "Who is that? Who is that talking?"

He paused for a long heartbeat before he replied, "It's 911. She's been shot."

I slammed the phone closed, tossed it into the passenger side of the car, tires screaming out of the parking lot. My office was about three miles away from the house on a double-lane highway, Route 50. Both a major through street and one accessing lots of shopping, it's a busy road, especially toward evening as rush hour kicked in.

And there are lots of stoplights, lots of stoplights that I missed in my furious dash to get home as soon as possible. My brain just couldn't conceive of what would happen if I didn't get there and get there right now.

I was laying on the horn. The sunroof was open though dusk was overtaking us quickly, and I was frantically gesturing to other cars to get out of the way with my right hand poking out of the car's roof. I was zigging and zagging between lanes and even nudging into the shoulder to move ahead, until I was utterly stopped about a half mile from the turnoff to my street. I was yelling and slamming my hands on the steering wheel, honking the horn like a mad woman, but I couldn't move forward.

With a split second decision, I turned the wheels to the left onto the median dividing my direction of travel from oncoming traffic. I pushed onto the grass, forcing the car onto the landscaped divider, and accelerated into a small gap in the ongoing traffic, heading for a gas station across the street. It wasn't pretty or subtle -- taken by surprise, other drivers started laying on their horns -- but I made it to that service station parking lot, which had another exit onto the street where I could reach my house.

I saw three ambulances immediately as I crested the hill. My car was probably left in the middle of the street with the door open the keys in the ignition, so fast was I up out of the driver's seat and sprinting toward the house, professional high heels and all. The January evening was coming on to full winter dark, even if it was very warm for the season, and I could see light spilling out of the open front door. I saw uniformed police officers and paramedics. I saw yellow caution tape. But as I flew through the door, I didn't see Kaela.

"Where is my daughter?" I was screaming at this point, all politeness gone. "Where is my daughter?"

Several police officers attempted to step in front of me or grab my arm, but I barreled through into the kitchen. I saw Philip standing silhouetted against the dark of the windows to the backyard. He had taken off his jacket to reveal a white shirt. His shirt and his hands were covered in blood, and red smears on his face and hairline showed where he'd put his hands to his face. His eyes looked empty and shocked, even scared. They quickly met mine.

"Where's Kaela?" I shouted. "Tell me!"

His eyes drifted to the open door. I lunged to go through it, but a team of four or five officers tackled me, bringing me all way to the kitchen floor before I stopped struggling. They weren't trying to be violent, but I was. I needed to find my daughter. I need to help my daughter.

"Where is my daughter?" I sobbed, my cheek on the cool tile of the floor.

"She's being taken care of Ma'am."

"Let me go to my daughter!"

The officers shifted their grip and positions, allowing me to get to my knees. They still surrounded me, and the officer in front of me tried to calm me down. "Your daughter has suffered a gunshot wound, and the paramedics are working on her now," he said with a level tone. He met my eyes very directly, as if it was a technique for dealing with crises they taught at the Academy. "I know it's your daughter, but that's a crime scene. You can't go out there right now."

I was breathing in gasps and my face was hot and wet with tears although I didn't remember crying. I tried to breathe deeper, slower. With the officers still surrounding me, still wary of me, I was able to look up at Philip and ask what happened.

He put his hand in his hair and explained he'd rounded the corner of the kitchen like usual, heading outside. As he approached, he saw feet -- or rather, a pair of shoes -- that he knew were Kaela's and wondered if she was sunbathing. It was a strangely warm afternoon for January, in the mid 70's. He was going to go out and tell her to go do her homework, but as he opened the door, "Something was wrong," he whispered hoarsely. "She was flat on the ground, and there was blood. I tried to do CPR." He gestured to his shirt to explain. "And there was David, next to her," he continued. "And they were both bleeding."

"David?" I sobbed. "What? David?"

"I don't know. I don't know," he replied.

It had been less than five minutes since Philip had called and I'd taken off in a storm. Only five minutes. My baby daughter was out on that deck bleeding right at that moment. Shot.

"Let me go," I demanded, rising to my feet.

The officers stayed close, and the one who spoke to me before said, "You want to let the paramedics work on her. Are you going to stop this if we let you go?"

I nodded my assent, but he nonetheless stayed between me and the door to the deck. But I did the unexpected. I pivoted on my foot and ran the opposite way out of the kitchen and into the adjoining family room, where there was a large picture window looking out on the deck. I heard voices calling after to me to stop, but by the time they caught up, I was standing at the window with my hands to my mouth, fingers interlaced, watching the scene outside.

The porch lights were on, though the emergency workers might have had additional flashlights or such. Yes, there was another body to the left and two-white shirted paramedics swarming over it, but I paid no attention. My gaze honed directly in on my barely 15-year-old daughter who lay bleeding into the wood planks of the deck. I could see most of her body in profile and there were two EMTs, one at her head with an oxygen mask and one kneeling at her chest performing CPR on her heart.

*She is still alive.* That was my first thought.

But I continued to look and saw the wound, or at least the effects of it if not the details. With every compression of her chest, the puddle of blood around her head surged slightly, growing larger. A head wound, a large head wound. Their efforts were simply pushing more of her lifeblood onto the deck. I saw her feet twitch a little, whether because of the action of the CPR or on her own, I didn't know. She spat up a bit, some bubbles forming at her mouth as the paramedic removed the oxygen from her face. Her eyes were closed, and remained closed. And then they sat back on their heels around her body, the firm voice commands they exchanged during the process ceasing, silence rising on their side of the glass and ours.

I must have stood there a little more than 20 seconds of their work when they stopped, then pulled a sheet up over Kaela's face, changing her status from a little and breathing teenager into a bulking white mass in the fading twilight. And then she was just a dead body. *My little daughter is now nothing but a dead body.*

I saw continued motion to my left. A collapsible stretcher was wheeled up and out, taking away David, if that's who it was. I paid little attention.

*

My daughter Kaela was dead. I knew that Kaela was dead. She'd been taken away in an ambulance to the hospital, but the sheet over her head was evidence enough that nothing could be done there to revive her. None of that made me yearn any less to be with her, to jump in a car and follow right behind the ambulance that carried her body, if not her soul. I wanted nothing more than to be near her, because she was still my daughter, alive or not, and I had not yet gotten accustomed to the idea that she was no longer alive.

Instead of following that ambulance as my heart desired, called to it as if by an unrelenting magnetic force, my house and the police officers that swarmed within it kept me hostage inside the walls. All the lights were on, and the house blazed like a beacon for tragedy in the dark night. There were uniformed and plain-clothes officers, technicians in scrubs with bags and cameras, and everywhere people taking notes or placing things in plastic bags. I resisted the flashes back to my childhood home where a similar scene followed my father's death.

The main details of the crime were finally related to me in bits and pieces. There was one gun, which David was holding when police arrived. He had apparently shot my daughter and then turned the gun on himself, dealing two fatal wounds.

My home was a crime scene, and in the eyes of the authorities, I was a main source of evidence about that crime, and I was not allowed to leave until I had aided the investigation.

Where had my daughter been that day? School, as far as I knew.

What had her mood been like lately? Good. Normal. I think. I don't know.

How long had she known David Kemps? What was the nature of their relationship? Are there any guns in the house? Did Kaela have any behavioral or emotional problems? Was she struggling at school? Had she changed her behavior in any drastic way?

"Why are you asking me about Kaela's behavior?" I asked. "She didn't shoot anyone. She was shot! She was shot! Isn't that enough without all of this?"

The officer leveled his gaze with mine, took a breath and then leveled with me. "It appears that Kaela was a willing participant in the shooting. She knelt before the boy, the shooter. She -- "

"That doesn't mean anything," I yelled. "He could have forced her. He could have overpowered her or . . . anything."

"That is a possibility," the officer admitted. "But we have to look into all avenues in ordcr to find out what really happened."

I did my best to answer all of their questions, but searching through my mind for such details was difficult. My brain was stuck on the present moment and the violence of it, the life-changing violence of the here and now. And yet they wanted me to think about the past, to talk about what had happened and what had been. I burst into tears several times. I began to question my own answers. How had she and David been connected or communicating at the time of the shooting? I didn't know. Did I have any reservations about this boy? Of course!

As for Kaela's behavior, was there something sinister or ominous recently that I'd missed? Had I misread any of her actions or words? How did this happen?

I kept thinking of her joyous face as she held up her autographed jersey just the night before. She was filled with elation, filled with life. She was so excited to be alive – animated and overjoyed that Bret Favre had spoken kindly to her, acknowledged her years of devotion, and signed her jersey for her, and that she could share that with her family. As she got into her bed last night and snuggled into her warm blankets, she wasn't planning to kneel down before a lovesick executioner and voluntarily let him put a bullet in her head. As she had shouted out her playful "I love you" chorus several times just a few hours earlier, she wasn't contemplating ending her life in some sort of dysfunctional Romeo and Juliet scenario. None of what they were implying seemed possible.

Over the course of the next two hours I watched the authorities dismantle a huge portion of Kaela's life. They removed her computer for evidence, all of her journals and school papers, her backpack and her address book. They were knee deep in the gathering of evidence when one of the officers finally found a note from Kaela. Kaela's note. Kaela's so-called suicide note.

It was taped to a cabinet in the hallway between the garage and Philip's office, a place where anyone coming into the house through the garage -- as we usually did -- would likely see it. Dozens of people had walked by it dozens of times, but at that moment, I happened to look up and see it taped there as if it was lit up by a sunbeam. O*h, my God!*

I reached out for it and just as my fingertips almost reached the paper a gloved hand of a policeman beat me to it. He snatched the note away, babbling about preserving evidence.

"Don't you see? I don't care about your preservation of evidence!" I whispered angrily, the loudest level at which I could speak with my throat constricted with emotion.

"But, ma'am," he said. "You can't touch it. We can't have you touching it."

I wanted to punch him in the mouth that he could say such things; it was my dead daughter's communication to me, a voice of comfort or explanation from beyond the veil . . . but I took a deep breath. "Fine, I won't touch it," I said. "But I am her mother, and I have a right to read that note. I am going to read that note right now in this house before you take it anywhere, even if that means you have to turn the pages for me."

He looked as if he was going to refuse, but he glanced at one of the other officers and got a small nod. We walked over to the counter in the kitchen. He laid the note out, several hand-written pages in Kaela's script. I glanced down to start reading, but my eye landed to the right of the page, where there was a silver gun -- the gun used to end my daughter's life, I had to assume -- lying casually on the countertop beside me.

I froze in shock and then grew angry. I glared at the officer and pointed, and he quickly had someone spirit the weapon away in a plastic bag. Still, the counter seemed to throb with the resilient presence of the weapon of destruction, as if it had left behind a scorched, invisible silhouette in space and time. An officer attempted to apologize, saying something about the gun being kicked away by Philip when he tried CPR, and then set to the side by a paramedic, and they were ever so sorry. He seemed genuinely sorry, and I genuinely didn't care.

*Let him feel bad. It's nothing in comparison to the way I feel at this moment.*

I tried to read the note along with the officer, fighting for focus because my eyes were blurry with tears. The rambling eight pages spoke about my husband Philip, about how he once tried to hit her, how he had made her mother (me) miserable and that she would hate him forever. She railed about her sister Niki tattling on her about something. She talked about how she didn't feel like anyone respected her wanting to live her life the way she wanted to, would never let her be. Then there were the honey-drenched sections to the people she loved, such as sending all her love to her BFF Shay. My forehead wrinkled as I read, because this letter was anything but a suicide note. In some ways it would have been almost comical, like the cutsie messages that teenagers write in the back of each other's yearbooks, if it hadn't been so tragic.

At the end of the missive, she'd signed the note Kaela Lynn Kemps. Kemps was David’s last name, of course.

I was allowed to read the entire thing before it was spirited away as evidence, but I certainly didn't understand it, let alone digest it or find any logic behind it. It wasn’t a suicide note . . . not one that I had ever heard about anyway. It was more of a runaway note it seemed to me. It seemed that she was telling us her reasons for running away with her boyfriend, the man that she was choosing to spend the rest of her life with.

At that point, I just glazed over and became like the living dead, present physically but not mentally as they asked me more and more inane questions. As helpful as a stone, I was finally allowed to leave the house and drive down to the hospital, where my daughter -- or what was left of her -- was waiting for her mother.

By the time we arrived, Kaela had already been taken to the morgue. I would not be able to see her again until arrangements could be made to move her to a funeral home. I tried to make those arrangements with my cell phone, but seemed only able to relay instructions to Philip and my friend Tina, who had arrived to offer support. About 15 minutes after we arrived, a nurse came to tell us that "the boy" was also dead and that they had not yet been able to contact his parents. I told them the contact information that I knew.

Parents. *Kaela's parents*. I realized I hadn't yet called Kaela's fatehr, Steven. He'd only just flown back from Wisconsin the night before, but that already seemed like so long ago. How was I going to tell him this? I had no idea, but I knew it was the first phone call I needed to make. Right then.

I flipped open the phone and took a deep breath. When he arrived on the line, I said, "I'm afraid I have some awful news. Kaela . . . ." My voice broke. "There's been a horrible accident in which Kaela was hurt."

He gasped and asked questions, but I couldn't answer. I just sobbed and shook my head, even if he couldn't see the motion.

"Just come to the hospital okay?" I said. I suddenly understood how Philip had felt when he couldn't relay the truth to me over the phone, the awful weight of the truth. I hated to lie to Steven, to withhold the part that our daughter was dead, but it was all I could do say, "Just come."

It wasn't until 3 o'clock in the morning that we arrived back home from the hospital, not at all tired or in any condition to go to sleep, but unable to do any more good in that brightly lit, sanitized shell of a building where my daughter's body was entombed. The house was a disaster. Not only had the police stomped in and out with their footprints and their caution tape and their evidence equipment . . . Not only had they stripped away so many elements that I was used to seeing in their appointed places . . . They also hadn't cleaned up the actual mess of the shooting on the back deck. My friend Tina was kind enough not to tell me that fact that night, simply keeping me out of the kitchen and away from the scene until the next day, by which time she could hopefully arrange for me never to have to see it. Or rather, see it again, this time without the paramedics or the crowds or the noise or the hope. Because I had no hope.

As I walked into the living room I noticed that the answering machine was blinking that we had new calls. My finger on the play button, I was dreading hearing messages from friends and family who had heard the news and wanted to give their condolences. I was in no condition to receive condolences. Instead, I stumbled upon the last thing I expected.

The robotic voice of the machine said the time the message was left that afternoon, then began playing the sound of Kaela's voice. The room became so quiet that I believe we could hear the beating of one another's hearts.

> Hey Mom, it's Kaela. It's three-twenty-five on Monday,
>
> January third. David is in our house right now with me. And,

> if you've walked through the garage, you probably know what happened.

I looked toward the garage at that point, confused and frustrated. Her voice up to that point seemed normal, if a little stressed, like many a message she'd left on this machine or on my voicemail over the years. Then her voice cracked with emotion and her words became somewhat blurry with sobs.

> I'm sorry that it has to be this way. You just won't let me get anything past you. I want to tell you that I'm sorry, and that I love you, and I'm sorry it came to this. Bye.

I sank to the floor like the bones suddenly abandoned my body, put my head in my hands and felt the first of what was a monstrous reservoir of tears begin to flow.

# Chapter Eleven

It was in the hours and days and even weeks after Kaela's death that what truly happened that violent January afternoon came to light. From the school, it was discovered based on Kaela's presence in some classes and absence in others that David had picked her up early, at about 10:30 in the morning. Also of note was that David, whether before he picked up Kaela or afterward, had withdrawn all the funds he had in the bank, all the money he could get his hands on immediately. However they had spent the intervening hours between mid morning and late afternoon, the only clues were in the physical evidence of my family home, which the police went over with a fine-tooth comb.

Starting at the top, upstairs in Kaela's room they found a packed suitcase, which was obviously a sign that she was considering leaving home, going away somewhere. The fact that they had stopped to withdraw money from David's back account would support that probability. However, the luggage never seemed to find its way further than that, left abandoned on the bed in her room. The only item usually in her room that did travel down the stairs was Cinnamon Bear, the stuffed toy animal that had been close to her heart since she'd had her first traumatic surgery years before. It was the bear that I knew she turned to when she was unsure or frightened, a comforting presence to her like a baby blanket or other memento can be for other scared kids. Kaela would never have left Cinnamon Bear behind, no matter where she was going. Cinnamon Bear was in the garage, however, obviously dropped in a moment when something unexpected had occurred, without the opportunity to recover him.

It was clear that David and Kaela had been in the garage. There were dusty footprints all over the concrete floor, trailing to and from the door of the house to different places in the garage. There would have been only one car present at the time with both Philip and I gone, a nice and (for a teenager, certainly) alluring Jaguar, giving them plenty of open space to walk around. That was traditionally the area where we kept most of the household tools, including dangerous items like gasoline for the lawnmower and combustible paint. Of more sentimental interest were boxes with holiday decorations, mementos from my daughters' childhood and, most visibly because of their size, a large amount of my personal artwork. Although I didn't draw regularly at the time, it was still an occasional release for me. Plus, I would always have a strong emotional connection to my past work, which was very important to me.

Here the police found what was the next step in the evidence chain: the gun case. The gun had belonged to David's father, also named David, though it seemed he had bought it at a gun show rather than through a dealer. It was a government-issue model with the serial number rubbed off. A hand gun, but a large one that would never have felt manageable in my own hands. On the dusty floor was the case, a hard-sided lockable case of the type many gun-owning homeowners use for safety, open on the ground lying in the dust. Beside it lay a box of ammunition.

It was obvious that something went on in that garage. The last remnants of my child's voice had said so: *If you've walked through the garage, you probably know what happened.* Pieces of the puzzle were missing, though, because I didn't immediately know what had happened. Neither had Philip when he arrived home that day. The garage told no obvious story about "what happened." The police and I could think of only two options.

For one, maybe David and Kaela were going to take the car and run away, leave their families, find some place to live together until Kaela was old enough to marry him under the law. Perhaps they thought they could get away with eloping right away somehow. There was that waiting Jaguar. Right inside the door, in the drawers of the hallway desk, were the spare keys. Plus, above that desk was the place we found Kaela's note taped to a cabinet. Could that have been why I would know what had happened when I came home as usual through the garage? The car would have been gone, and then we would have seen the keys gone and her note, all in a neat line. The packed suitcase waiting to be carried down and put into the trunk, Cinnamon Bear carried out to the waiting Jaguar, and David and Kaela dropping by to withdraw his money from the bank. It made sense, a certain amount of comforting sense, though it could not and never can be proved.

If that was the plan, it was obviously just the version that David had allowed Kaela to believe, up until that certain point. The insertion of the pistol into the scene would have been a surprise, resulting in the dropped and abandoned Cinnamon Bear, left lying face down in the dust of the garage floor. Nothing in my experience allows me to believe that she would have just dropped and left Cinnamon Bear there voluntarily.

The second theory was that the garage was the original location they'd thought of to carry out their violent plans. This, too, made some sort of sense, because the garage was a place where the inevitable mess could be easily cleaned up and leave no lasting damage. I can picture that idea going through my thoughtful daughter's head, that her mother was a neat freak slightly over the line into cleanliness obsession, which I would not be able to handle the debris of her death soaking into the carpet or spattering a wall. If you're planning your own death, being considerate about such things seems like an afterthought, but I knew that to be true. That she didn't want to hurt me in any way she didn't have to.

Perhaps she looked around to see all the dangerous and flammable chemicals that could be ignited by a stray bullet. Perhaps it was the thought of destroying my art or any of the precious memoirs of the rest of the family. Perhaps it was simply hot and stuffy, because it was an unseasonably warm day. Whatever the reason, the suitcase was left upstairs and the gun case and bear were left behind in the garage, along with their plans, whatever they might have been, and they went through the house ending up on the back deck.

The deck was slightly elevated over the green grass of the backyard, which wasn't exceptionally large, a plot of turf about the size of a typical living room. A fence divided us from two nearby neighbors. The neighbor directly to the back was a man who worked from home, who had his window open to air the indoor stuffiness with the warm winter air. To the right was a nice young couple, the wife pregnant and in the kitchen next to our yard, washing and putting away dishes.

Between 3 and 4 o'clock in the afternoon, Kaela was on the deck. She had a bottle of water nearby, which seems odd to me, if at such a tense and dramatic time to stop for a drink of water. It doesn't seem like thirst would be a top priority had she known the plan. She also had the ring she'd told me she found near the bus stop months earlier on the third finger of her left hand, on her wedding ring finger. That should have made sense to me a long time ago, that such a "found" item could hardly be unimportant to her, as insignificant as she took pains to make it seem to me.

By force or by volition, Kaela knelt down in front of David facing away from the house. The police have told me that such an action reveals that she went along with him, that wanted to die, that she intentionally committed suicide by the act of bending at the knee. *Do people who are executed not kneel when their murderers threaten them?* I thought. That is what happened from any possible perspective. She was executed, whether she willingly participated or not. She knelt and David, her on-again-off-again boyfriend of more than a year, shot her in the back of the head.

This bullet passed through Kaela and continued its trajectory toward the neighbor's house, through a drainpipe and the wall and into the kitchen of the pregnant mother, where it lodged in a corner between two cabinets. She was unharmed, and in fact, was completely unaware that the deadly projectile had invaded her space. She'd been unloading clean dishes from the dishwasher and placing them back in the cabinets. She did hear a noise, but not a gunshot. She thought that perhaps a glass recently put back into a closed cabinet had tipped over. A small clunk.

David then turned the gun around and shot himself. Likely because of the angle of the shot, the bullet was never recovered by police, at least not that I'm aware of. What they did find on the body, however, was David's personal suicide note. It wasn't left out where anyone could find it, including Kaela. It was, instead, folded several times and placed tightly against his wrist, held in place with a yellow, rubber bracelet that said Livestrong, distributed by the Lance Armstrong Foundation. The bracelets were very popular at the time, but that made the situation no less ironic. Living strong in murder-suicide?

In David's suicide letter, which was more of an angry rant at his parents and the world than a straight-forward letter, he said that he hated the mother who had left him years ago. He wrote more vitriol about his father, interspersed with lots of four-letter words. And of course, he said that he believed if he and Kaela "couldn't be together in this life, we will be together forever in heaven." It was a straight-forward declaration of his intention to commit suicide and the reason behind it, unlike Kaela's rambling missive. The latter, while certainly angry with some people, did not drip with self-hatred and venom and violence in the way that David's words -- strapped to his lifeless wrist that caused the violence -- did.

And somewhere in that vague timeline of events, Kaela had called me, had made a point of leaving a message just for me, her mother. And in that message she'd said that she was leaving me and she said that she loved me. Loved, but left. My brain whirled around those two contradictory thoughts, too knotty and emotional for me to untangle right away.

And yet there were somehow still questions for the authorities to ask of me, her overwhelmed and overemotional mother. Some were repetitions of the same questions, others were variations on a theme, but all were related to Kaela's recent behavior. Had they worked out whatever was their initial plan was while she was at her father's house, before she had left?

But she was so happy to get back, so happy to see me, so happy to tell me and the world all about Brett Favre. She'd been a normal girl, probably a more than normal girl. She was on the debate team and tutored other kids. She babysat after school and aided the school swim team. Her teachers said that rather than slipping academically as suicide kids do, Kaela was the type to make sure every T was crossed and ever I dotted, going over and above what was asked for in assignments. She wasn't gaining or losing weight, or moping, or giving away her possessions to her friends. She didn't seem fatalistic to anyone.

All the police officers and other investigators, of whom there were so many that I lost track, said, "She doesn't fit the profile. She just doesn't fit the profile." And yet, they continued to ask.

*

When the sun finally rose on the day following Kaela's death, I knew immediately in my heart that this day I was opening my eyes upon was the first day without her. At least yesterday had briefly known her, seen her face. She'd breathed the air of yesterday. This new day would never be aware of the existence of my younger daughter, nor would any day for the rest of eternity, even though I forever would.

That's likely the most coherent thought about the actual violent event that I formed in the few days afterward. There were too many practical things to do.

First of all, I had to arrange for all the accoutrements of death for my youngest, my 15-year-old daughter, a task I never dreamed I would have to complete and was quite unprepared for. The hospital and hospital morgue had held my hand through the steps of calling a funeral home and having her body moved, but where would she be moved after that? Where should we make Kaela's final resting place? We set out to find a cemetery and a plot within it for her grave.

Even less than 24 hours after her death, I knew I wanted to get away from our house in South Riding, which had been Kaela's last home – the crime scene. It was a vague feeling, not localized into action, but more of an idea of wanting to get in a car and drive away. Kaela's reference to Philip in her final note had also planted a seed in my head. She wrote that she would forever hate him, in part because he made her mother miserable and that she would never forgive him for that.

Was I miserable? Was I miserable yesterday, before the chaos, because of him? Would I be more miserable now because of him? I couldn't tell, but the roots of the idea had been planted and therefore I knew that I didn't mind at all -- and might perhaps prefer -- for my daughter's burial place to be a bit of a distance from our neighborhood.

We found the ideal place about 10 miles away in a cemetery called Stonewall Memorial Gardens that had the atmosphere I was looking for: no new construction, no high-rise buildings and a low crime rate. It just seemed peaceful all around with mature trees and well tended grass. Flowers and other items left by families made the area seem loved and oft visited. Philip, Niki and I made the trip together and were met by a helpful, considerate grief counselor who led us through the process. We were shown several plots dotted all around the large facility, most with different drawbacks. One was obviously too close to the border, where there would be more noise and activity. Another had far too much vegetation, making it seem messy.

Then the counselor said, "I have a few plots over in this area that you might like. There are several openings there that are lovely."

"How many?" Philip asked. I looked at him with my head tilted, wondering why it mattered. "I've been thinking that we should be looking for a set together, for Kaela and for us, to plan for the future."

The thought shocked me. I hadn't really thought about anything but finding a resting spot for my daughter, who had been through so much and needed that rest. I hadn't thought about the rest of the family. I had up to that point never given a thought to where I would like to be buried, let alone to actually pre-purchasing the plot.

"Three, I think," said Philip. "Niki will likely get married and have a family of her own, and she'll probably want to think about all this stuff with them. She won't want to be buried out here with her mom. Niki? Does that sound about right?"

Her eyes puffy and her hair disarrayed with grief, Niki shrugged and nodded.

"So you, me and Kaela," Philip said to me, and he said it in front of this stranger, the counselor and Niki. "We'd need three plots."

My heart was beating hard, trying to get out of the situation somehow, but my head wasn't thinking clearly. *So much had changed. Would Philip and I change, too? Did I want Philip and I to change, too? Did I want to be married to him, lying beside him even in death?* I didn't know my own mind, as emotional as I was, and he seemed so sure, sure enough to broadcast it in front of other people. I didn't want to make a scene. We'd had enough of scenes in the last 48 hours. So I went along with his suggestion, even if my beating heart was trying to tell me that something was wrong.

These plots were all the way near the back fence. "The cemetery is actually a historic battleground, and so nothing commercial will ever be built behind here," the counselor explained.

There was a large, spreading tree, its leaves dappling the sunshine and making a comforting rustling whisper in the wind. The air was sweet and slightly cool with the tree's shade, and the area all around that part of the cemetery seemed both clean and peaceful. I hadn't really known what I was looking for up to that point, but clean and peaceful seemed to hit the nail on the head. It was the perfect spot to lay to rest a young girl whose end had been violent and messy.

There were three plots together in front of that grandmother tree, which seemed to guard and watch over the charges in her care. Very few of the other plots were currently filled, but we took those three, signed on the dotted line and began to arrange for the day of her internment, directly after the funeral. Such counselors, accustomed as they are to death and grief, are always very kind and considerate, even more so when you're mourning the death of a child. She made every detail as easy as possible, right down to choosing the headstone and the inscription I wanted engraved on it while my head and thoughts were blurry with tears.

We were a Methodist family, and the church was just as helpful in setting up the memorial service. While my memories of the event are jumbled and steeped in grief, I vividly remembered the pastor's speech, given over a coffin piled with flowers. The audience was large -- lots of Kaela's friends and classmates were also hit hard by the unexpected tragedy -- and often loud with sobs and cries. But he stood there in his white and black vestments, his eyes wise and calm, and spoke about those feelings left behind by death.

"It's only human when people you love die, when you're upset and grieving," he said, "especially when the cause of that death is so tragic . . ." He paused, not wanting to talk about suicide, but letting the audience soak in his meaning more gently. "It's only human to feel waves of guilt or blame wash through you. You ask, 'What did I do that this happened? What didn't I do that could have prevented this from happening? Why did it have to happen at all?'"

I choked on my tears, his words expressing exactly some of the thoughts and emotions roiling through me at that moment.

"Instead," the pastor continued, "I want you to think about how wonderful this bright and beautiful young girl was, as so many of you have told me in your own words. She was so very special, helpful, always wanting to help others. Instead of dwelling on our loss or the reason for our loss, let us think about God's gain and the reason for it. He never said that she would be ours forever. He knew her talents, and he needed Kaela with him now. Therefore, death makes her no less special, bright and beautiful, and no less loved."

His words were touching and wise and they were etched into my brain for me to read over repeatedly in times of distress. But while those words told me that questions -- *Why, dear God? Why?* -- were in vain, I could not stop asking them because I had no answers.

The internment, too, went smoothly despite the grief that emanated from the funeral cluster like a thick, choking fog. I was supported on one side by Niki and the other side by Steven, my ex-husband. My current husband Philip stood to the side throughout the day and through most of the planning, leaving everything to me. Steven glanced at him with loathing a few times over the course of the day, but emotions were running high all around.

After the brief ceremony that saw Kaela's body safely cradled in the ground, we walked as a group toward the cemetery's office. I was shaky in my black high heels, and Philip dragged along a few steps behind Steven, Niki and me. We met with our counselor to finish up the process once and for all.

"Don't worry," she said, a comforting hand on my shoulder. "This is the final stage."

We double checked the completed headstone and scheduled a time for it to be erected. Steven and I handled the final payment. As the counselor took the check, I mused out loud, generally in Philip's or Niki's direction, "I wonder where David Kemps, the boy, will be buried?"

One of the other counselors was nearby and gently stepped up to our chairs. "Actually, he's going to be buried here, Ma'am."

"Excuse me?"

Our counselor stood up and went to confer with her colleague, then returned with her mouth compressed, turned down at the corners.

"Apparently, the Kemps were here the day after I helped you with your arrangements," she said, "working with another counselor. He's to be buried here."

"Excuse me? Where?" I demanded.

"Less than a dozen spaces away from your daughter."

I almost fainted. *Can we move her?* I don't know if I said it out loud or not. It was too late, either way, I knew.

*So now they really would be together forever.* I wasn't aware that my broken heart could fracture into even smaller pieces.

*

Even before the funeral, the local news had been referring to David and Kaela's death as a "Romeo and Juliette" killing. All four regional news stations pulled their satellite vans with towering antennae up to our house the very night of the shooting and filmed evening remote broadcasts with our lawn with the flashing lights of police cars and ambulances in the background. For the next week, there was at least one of the vans emblazoned with the TV station's initials pulled up to the curb. When knocking on the door or ringing the bell to ask for an interview didn't work, persistent reporters would push microphones in my face as I entered or left the house, even going so far as to run up to one of our cars as we attempted to drive away.

I had never realized how voyeuristic people were. Apparently, unforeseen tragedy that could befall any family in America is the type of story that is particularly attractive. Happy and safe in their own homes, people can *tut tut* about how sad it was for us, all the time feeling a little better because at least that didn't happen to them. At least their lives weren't quite that messed up.

I tried to tune out all the coverage that I could, but I couldn't help but catch some of the news they broadcast on TV. It was a major story for days, evolving from reporters finding out the details of what had happened, then delving into Kaela and David's history, their relationship and their school. Finally, it became a story about how national trends of suicide were playing out in our own backyard, as if my daughter was little more than evidence of a statistic. They flashed suicide helpline numbers and listed signs of suicidal behavior across the screen.

One evening I saw our home behind one of the reporters as she talked into her microphone and gestured behind her at key moments for effect. There was a faint movement in the background and then a tiny orange glow. I looked, trying to focus on what that might be in front of my house. *That's Philip!* I thought. *That's Philip outside smoking a cigarette.* I ran to the front door, stuck only my arm out and grabbed his shoulder, pulling him back inside.

Calls for interviews poured in all day every day for the first week, and we often wouldn't answer the phone. I didn't give very many interviews myself, only one that seemed to be writing a piece of some value to me or to Kaela's memory. For the most part, Philip, Niki (who was pretty much camping out with at the house instead of at her apartment) and I just answered "no comment" to anyone in the media asking for information or opinion.

Nonetheless, I learned a great deal about the day of the shooting itself and about David Kemps through some of that subsequent media coverage.

When I had first met David, I thought about him as a prankster and a joker, someone lighthearted and silly. Especially when I just knew him as a local kid who worked at Food Lion, he seemed like a character with a big sense of humor, and to a certain degree, I admired how far he would take some of his jokes. When he started to pursue my daughter -- I think of it as pursuing rather than dating -- he immediately seemed more serious and dangerous in my eyes. The newspaper and the radio were now revealing that I really had no idea.

According to his former teachers, friends and classmates, he was a loner who was a bit isolated from his peers. He was never very popular with girls and his grades and classroom participation left a lot to be desired. He was in "college," as I'd known, but it was a school with low admission requirements where he continued to be a mediocre student, again uninvolved with the classes or many other students. He was not unattractive, actually somewhat handsome, but it seemed like he had an immature intensity that scared off a lot of girls his own age. I knew that girls of Kaela's age, however, weren't looking for the same things in a boy and didn't ask the same questions that young college women considering a life-long mate were. She was awed at the fact that he was in "college," or even just the fact that he had his own vehicle, although it was just an old beat up pick-up, and he lavished attention on her, who was so much younger. Only young women in their twenties start thinking seriously and discriminately about where a boy is going in life, what his goals are, what he wants from life, and why he is so resentful or angry at the world.

The *London Times* from Britain happened to be doing an in-depth story about suicide around the time of Kaela's death, and they choose their tragedy as a case study to highlight. A nice young reporter had flown over from London, and though I gave her a short interview, David's family refused to speak with her at all. Nonetheless, the resulting article framed the situation in a way I hadn't consciously put together before. The reporter noted that Kaela came from an upper class home, describing our custom home, new cars and such. Then she spoke about David's home as a "working class, clapboard house" in a less posh neighborhood. She definitely saw the social differences between them that I suppose I hadn't made conscious note of. David's father had helped him use some of his money earned to get a truck and chipped in some of the costs to help. Even at 15, Kaela had almost $8,000 of her own money saved for her first car. Then there were the academic differences: He was a mediocre student, while she excelled at school and enjoyed doing so.

To me, it seemed to paint a picture of a young man who was mad at the world and his place in it, but who was nonetheless enamored of a young woman who seemed to have the best that the world had to offer. She had what he wanted, and he couldn't get it in a normal, socially acceptable way. It seemed like the story of the naive being snared by the manipulative.

Obviously, not everyone saw it the same way that I or the *Times* did. They continued to call it a double suicide. They continued to insist that my Kaela was just a typical teen suicide. They hadn't seen her lit up face just hours before the bullet exploded from the barrel of David's gun. Even the coroner had officially put the cause of death on her death certificate as suicide, so I had not gone to pick it up. I said I never would as long as it contained that word, a word too simplistic for the truth of the matter.

Of course, the Kemps, too, were upset. I would never expect them not to be. No matter what I had once thought of David as a romantic attachment for my daughter or thought now that he had killed her, the fact remained that they lost a son that they loved. I knew that their pain must approach my own. However, David's father and step-mother didn't seem to be grieving in solitude, because both of them made it publicly obviously that they blamed our family for what had happened to their son. Or rather, they blamed *me* specifically. They proclaimed that their poor boy was a victim.

They began to give interviews and make statements on the news that I had driven "the kids" to suicide because I forbade their love, that if only I'd let them be together that they'd be happy and in love still. The truth was that when the police searched the Kemps' house after the shooting -- just as they had searched through Kaela's belongings for evidence -- they found several other guns and ammunition, accessible to David and perhaps even to his six-year-old sister. Without access to David Sr.'s weapons, obviously the crime couldn't have occurred, but the Kemps family didn't see it that way at all.

A few days after their deaths, there was a candlelight vigil for David and Kaela attended by their friends and classmates and many people in the community. There were two big banners that mourners could sign leaving messages for the kids. I was a mess at the time, too upset to attend, but David Sr. was there. He stood beside his son's tribute banner where the kids filed up to use markers to sign them, and several people later told me that he repeatedly said to those coming up to sign, "I'm sorry you have to sign this. You wouldn't have had to if that bitch had just let them be together like they wanted. They wouldn't be dead now."

His step-mother also talked to what seemed like everyone in the town, because friends and other parents often told me about how she went on and on about how I should feel the weight of two deaths on my guilty shoulders. I even started to receive hate mail. David Kemps, Sr. began to patrol near our house every night after dark, driving slowly and creepily by the driveway and staring in the windows, his eyes flashing in the streetlights. It was so frightening that I was forced to call the police several times. I didn't want to press charges or anything like that. I just wanted them to tell him to knock it off. In some ways the situation was even more creepy than if it had been someone else doing nighttime drive-bys, because David Sr.'s behavior seemed to eerily mimic that of his son: persistent, volatile and threatening.

There was also a tidal wave of sympathy from family, friends, distant acquaintances and even people we didn't know. Flowers overflowed from room to room, creating a thick and sickly sweet pall in the house. I eventually had to line up the vases and baskets and garlands along the entire sunroom floor, but it seemed callous to throw even one away, even if I had no idea who the sender was. Maybe Kaela had known these people.

Food was also pouring in faster than we would ever have been able to eat it. Our freezer was full, as was our fridge and every countertop in the kitchen, piled high with casserole dishes, meat and cheese trays, and cakes. Niki and I finally made a list of different dishes we would hand over to the fridges of different neighbors. People, too, came and went almost without ceasing, it seemed to me. Faces, all these faces, either blurrily recognized through grief or completely foreign to me in the first place. I had never seen that amount of people come through my house in all the years we'd lived there. And it may sound terrible, but all I wanted was for them all to go home and leave me in peace.

But if everyone left, I would be alone with Philip, which was becoming an increasingly uncomfortable thought. As someone who had been abused as a child, I didn't recognize how he subtly and not so subtly manipulated me with controlling or abusive language or emotions. Things like insisting on three plots in front of an audience, forcing me to either make a scene or submit, then to write the check from my personal account. He'd not really helped with any of the arrangements, only tagging along to keep an eye on me, but not taking over with help or to give me a break when I so desperately need someone to take over for me. When we first met, he was struggling to make ends meet, was driving a beat up little car, and was tired of being an employee of someone else's business. Now he was running our consulting firm that my contacts in government had gotten started, with a large salary that he paid himself, and hoarded away instead of putting in the family coffers. His "me first" attitude had been an annoyance to me before, but I was beginning to wonder if I could so easily overlook it and similarly unflattering characteristics now.

As early as three days after Kaela's death I had approached Philip about wanting to move out of the house, which not only had so many wonderful memories of Kaela growing up, but that also now housed the awful memorizes of her final, violent moments. I was living in the murder scene, for god's sake. I couldn't stay there.

"No," he said, his tone neutral. "We built this house ourselves. I'm staying."

He glanced over his shoulder at me. I was on the couch with my legs tucked up underneath me dressed in pajamas and without make up. I had been forced into the rigid clothes of mourning all day most every day, forced to put on a face for the world around me, which kept prying into my grieving. But that was winding down now. The fire of interest was cooling in the media and in the area, and would die out almost entirely within another week or two.

"But, I just don't think I can stay here," I explained, not wanting to go into great detail about that which should be obvious. I was his wife. He should understand how hurt I was. I shut my eyes tight, but a tear managed to escape on each side of my nose.

"I guess," he shrugged. "I'll buy your half out then, if you want."

"What?" I took a deep breath in, but it became a rough sob. "How could you?"

"Well, go off and cry somewhere," he said, and left the room.

At that point, crying felt like it was all I had in me to do anyway. It seemed that Kaela had been right about Philip.

## Chapter Twelve

When Kaela died, obviously it was an instant life-changing event, a horrible tragedy that stops everyday life in its tracks. However, as the media coverage faded away and the weeks started to pass into a month, then two, it actually surprised me that life continued to go on, that the world continued to spin and people to go about their business as if nothing had happened.

Life goes on.

It's a platitude that every man, woman and child has heard, but it's a truth that still comes as a surprise when you see it happen. You see time ticking on and routines being observed, while somehow you sit motionless in the midst of it like a rapid in a fast-flowing river.

I think my obsessive nature was what at first drove me forward. There were details to arrange. There was a house to clean and food to cook. I've always relished routines. They made me feel stable and safe, imposing order and discipline on my life like both Ruby and the military had done in my past. I've always loved keeping things obsessively clean and well ordered, and it turned out that keeping up the pace to carry out those tasks allowed me to avoid confronting the turmoil that was going on in my head.

I wasn't confronting anything at that point. I felt like the real me had receded inside the shell of my body, becoming the mere controller of my body. I could look out through the eyes, make the hands go through the motions. I could even make the face smile or put on a mask of stoicism that I did not feel. But it wasn't the real me that was present in the world, only this drone I was operating by remote control. The real me -- the bundle of emotions and pain that was the real me -- hid away from the world, and even from me.

I was navigating this drone through a minefield, an emotional minefield. While the police had ruled the death a double-suicide and the Kempses were actively pointing their fingers at me in blame, I could not accept any of it as true. I would never accept that, and there were those people that agreed with me, including Niki.

One of the first things Niki said to me after Kaela's death was, "You know, she'd never do this to you."

"It just doesn't make sense," I agreed.

"No, it doesn't make sense," Niki said. "Mom, you guys were so close. I was jealous of how close you and Kaela were. I didn't think she'd ever do something like this to you; to us."

"But she did, Niki. She's dead, Niki."

"She would never do this," she repeated.

I went over and over the note Kaela had left behind, six pages of rambling. I couldn't get over the tone of it, that it reminded me of what teenagers write in a yearbook at the end of a school term, not what a teenager writes as she's ending her young and precious life: "To my BFF Shay: You always made me laugh." I went over the language with a fine-tooth comb. "This is the only way that David and I can be together." It was good-bye, but without the tone of finality that a suicide note would carry. It sounded like they were running away togetehr. Kaela's bags were packed. As of the moment she placed her clothes in that bag, she thought she was going somewhere, and she didn't need luggage to go to heaven, like David's hidden note had designated as his destination. Besides, if they really wanted to be together, couldn't they just have waited a few years? If what they felt was true love as Kaela claimed in the letter, it would still be there between them in three years when Kaela turned 18, when she reached the age of consent. Where did the impatience come from? That was not like Kaela at all.

I talked with Kaela's dad Steven about the letter extensively. The note was so lengthy that it seemed likely she'd not written it the day of the shooting, but perhaps while she was on vacation with her father. Steven lent credence to the idea, saying that Kaela had asked his mother for notepaper and a pencil at one point. Her grandmother thought she'd been writing a friend back home. Then Steven told me about an ominous phone call he'd overheard only days before he brought her back to Virginia. He walked by the room she was staying in and had glanced in to see her deep in conversation, the phone cradled between her ear and shoulder. Normal enough, but her face was bright red and she was crying. Her words were sharp and obviously upset. Steven made to come in the room to talk to her, but she waved him away and closed the door. She'd later appeared to be in a completely normal mood, so he'd chalked the incident up to the wacky hormones of teenage girls.

Afterward, we both knew that any incident that seemed normal and harmless at the time could have meant something, could have heralded the coming of this tragedy. Where else could the omens be found? I questioned. I made myself go through a methodical and mechanical search.

I started in her bedroom. The police had turned it upside down looking for evidence of what had happened, perhaps signs of foul play, but most of Kaela's things had been returned. I spent days putting the room back in order, putting everything in its place. Even though Kaela had been a typical messy teenager, my obsessive nature made it necessary to put her room to rights. I felt like I was preserving the space, as if she could walk back in any minute. I wanted her to walk back in and feel completely at home. I wanted her to see her room and be comforted, even if she was only seeing it looking down from heaven. It felt like the least I could do.

Of course when I was putting her things away, I saw Kaela's journals, where she wrote down most of her secrets and clandestine adventures, and crushes and dramas. She was pretty regular about writing in her journal, which I had always encouraged and had never attempted to violate her privacy to read. But she was gone now, so I took the liberty, looking for answers. I was searching for clues about what had happened to my daughter and why she was now dead.

In retrospect, it's a decision I deeply regret. If I had the chance to do things over again, I would have left my daughter's diaries alone and unopened. The pain of those diaries is still fresh. Granted, much of what Kaela wrote was benign and expected. She wrote about slumber parties and conversations with friends, about the big, dramatic cat fights that girls of that age have over the most trivial matters. But there was also a significant part of the journal that dealt exclusively with David, whom Kaela believed to be the love of her life. She dreamt about their future together, of marriage and children. She dreamt about what it would be like if I accepted him, how it would feel to invite him home for dinner with the family.

However, I also found out the extent to which my daughter was lying to me about her involvement with him, that she had never -- not once in all the times I thought I'd stopped the relationship -- truly broken it off with him. That struck me like a blow, that she'd gone to such lengths to deceive me, that she could be so devious. It revised my perspective of history and of her personality. She wrote at great lengths of all the methods she had employed to get away with the secret relationship, and I berated myself for being so naive and easy to fool.

Then there were the sections of text where Kaela talked about how mad she was at me, both in regard to the David situation and for other incidental matters. We all say and write awful things when we're upset that we later regret or no longer believe. But here were some nasty and mean-spirited things written about me, her mother, and now that she was dead, they were set in stone, as permanent and irreversible as the tribute I had engraved on her headstone. She would never live to revise those opinions. This, then, was what she thought of me. How could I have been so hard and cruel? How could I keep her apart from the man she loved? How much of that had just driven her closer to David?

I was too soft; I was too hard. I was too strict; I was not strict enough. The two thoughts may be diametrically opposed in the mature mind, but both seemed true in the hormonally driven youthful mind. Either way, I was at fault for the teenage feelings she was experiencing at any given moment as she penned her innermost emotions in her journal. It was a difficult pill for a surviving mother to swallow.

Even more difficult when reading her journals was knowing for certain that she and David had a sexual relationship. She had been a 14-year-old girl, early in her puberty, and he was a 19-year-old man, and he was taking full advantage of his added levels of sophistication and ability to manipulate her—which is why our society makes it a crime—because little girls are ill-equipped at that tender age to deal with the sexual advances of an older predator like this.

I'd had my suspicions that this might have been going on, of course, but seeing proof in my daughter's own hand was difficult for me to face. The very thing I had feared, that David would physically take advantage of this young girl illegally and immorally, had happened repeatedly. Folded up in the back of a journal was an unsent note to a friend that even said that Kaela briefly feared she had become pregnant. My little girl who was barely old enough to get a learner's permit to drive, seduced by a man in college. I couldn't help but weep and shudder at the thought, and I wished I could cleanse the information from my mind for all time.

It was obvious why David had made his decision that there were no other options. He was going down; he was going away, and he knew it. Had he told Kaela they could run away and make a life in Canada, where no one would question their union? Had he promised her that they could be husband and wife and start a little family? Had he oversold the dream of love and romance to a little girl, waking up one morning and realizing that there was no way he could avoid years in prison for what he had been doing to her? It was impossible to continue hiding their relationship, and they were getting in too far to even try to for much longer. The end of the *status quo* was drawing near, one way or another. His note was very clear about his end – he was going out in a blaze of glory and he was sure to send up the one-fingered salute to anyone who might be reading – and it was strapped to his body where Kaela couldn't see it. Kaela's note, however, like her packed bag and favorite stuffed bear, was out in the open, and spoke more of a new beginning with her true love than the end of a short life brought tragically and violently to an abrupt end.

The last entry was from the Friday before she died, which was on a Monday. If she had been planning to run away with David or to die with him, she didn't trust that information to even her journal. I was forced to confront more information about my daughter and perhaps more omens of the upcoming tragedy that I thought I could have seen, or should have seen. But I still had no answers.

I was afraid of the growing weight of guilt that was pulling at me, making me feel like I was walking upstream through life with thick mud dragging at my ankles. In cases of suicide, it's hard not to feel a sense of guilt. *What could I have done? Why couldn't she talk to me? Why didn't she ask for help? Why didn't I know something was desperately wrong?* Whether or not Kaela's death was suicide, the suggestion that it was made me feel as guilty as if it was.

More than a month after the shooting, I was walking from the bathroom of the house to the dining room. Perhaps it was the time of day or a certain trick of the light, but my eye caught on something wrong in my otherwise extremely tidy house. I walked up to look closer at a framed photo of Philip's mother hanging on the wall. There, on the tip of her nose, was a dried wad of white mashed potatoes, a remnant of one of those famous food fights that my girls and I enjoyed on occasion. It must have been there for months, if not for longer than a year.

As I wiped it off with a paper towel and some spray cleaner, I stopped in my tracks. *Is this how it's always going to be? Is her very existence going to be erased piece by piece just as I am wiping away this evidence of her having been here?*

The *me* inside myself seemed to be getting smaller and smaller, a hard marble rattling around in the empty shell, ricocheting and pinging like a pinball machine. It pulsed with caged energy, like the tiny speck of matter exploding into the big bang and creating the entire universe. And as it pulsed, it seemed to be telling me: *It's all your fault. It's all your fault*. It frightened me to my core, feeling that potential of awesome power, so I held on to the strings of my Lorijane puppet even tighter, making her get out of the bed in the morning, making her smile or nod her head when engaged in conversation.

I was acting like I was all right, trying to convince myself that if I tried long and hard enough, it would become okay. I even went back to work in the months after Kaela's death, going through the motions and putting on a mask of normalcy throughout the day. I was fighting whatever tide of emotion had started building in me after my daughter's death, fighting a losing battle.

Yes, I learned the truth of the platitude "life goes on." But then I came full force to the realization of another one: *No matter where you go, there you are*. There was to be no escape from that frightening me inside myself, waiting to overtake me, to overwhelm me.

There was a tipping point, I know there was, but I really can't identify the particular straw that broke the camel's back. I had been back at work for a while, going through the motions or normal living. When you work with the public a great deal, you kind of get used to putting on your "work face" in order to relate to customers and give them a positive experience. But my work face seemed thicker and heavier as the weeks rolled by. I began to think that I must look like a woman wearing far too much make-up, a clown face mask that was fooling no one.

I stopped to think. *Why fool them? Why care?*

As the tide turned, I gradually stopped trying to remain above water, seduced by the silence and peace of the deep pulling at my ankles. By the time the summer rolled around I was unable to work, unable to do almost anything but be overpowered.

*

What is a person worth? How do you divine their value? I've heard that you can break down the physical substance of the human body into its most basic elements, and that those essentials would sell for a couple of bucks in the modern marketplace. But there has to be more to it than that. Some people who are vitally important to one person could be negligible to someone else. Some people calculate their value through what the make with their hands or brains or the amount of money that they sock away, but those all seem like superficial and incomplete methods.

Instead, it seemed to me like people were defined and valued through the way they are treated by other people . . . by how many people love and care for them, and how many loathe and avoid them. It's really the only objective measure I could think of, and I thought about it a lot.

The more I thought, the more my own value seemed to boil down to only the watery elements that made up the cells of my body, nothing more, because I had not been treated well by many people. So many people had made it perfectly clear how worthless I was to them, how much they failed to recognize me as someone special – there was my dear mother, and all of her family; even my father had chosen death over life, a life that I could have enjoyed with him to some extent no matter what he had done; Steven had preferred the life at sea to a life in my warm embrace; and Philip, it was becoming quite clear that he had preferred the financial security I had offered and was not in a relationship with me for the love I offered; and even Kaela, my sweet baby Kaela . . . had she preferred death over a life with me? I was just a tiny speck of humanity, hardly worth noticing except to maybe shoo it away like an annoying housefly.

This latest tragedy in my life began to crack open the cement casing I'd poured around the tragedies of my past. The dam I'd constructed separating my childhood from the person I had built myself into began to split, and leak, until it finally burst and flooded over me. It all started to come back.

There was my mother ironing in the front room of my childhood house framed in the screen door, Michelle in the corner. There was the sound of the cast-iron frying pan hitting my brother across his skull, splitting open to what looked to me like the brain. I could feel her small yet incredibly strong hand in my hair, and I could taste the alum, and it stung.

*I never wanted any of you,* her voice screamed at me across the chasm of decades. *Yeah, you better run, you brat. I'm going to send you to foster care!*

I was at home now almost constantly and alone for most of that time. I rarely emerged from the bedroom, which had the permanent stuffiness of sleep in the air, and I spent long hours looking at the window and beyond to the neighborhood below. The neighbors coming and going, the cars and kids on bikes: they were like little ants or tiny toy soldiers, playthings.

And yet, this was what they called reality, the real world, all these smoke and mirrors and masks and pointless conversations and mind-numbing routines. How could they continue their silly and futile lives now that the grand comedy had been called to a halt? Hadn't they received the memo that life was over?

The world inside my head was what seemed real to me, growing to envelope the bedroom and the whole house and feeling much more tangible and frightening than anything those suburban streets or the "reality" beyond them could throw at me.

I relived my childhood feelings of worthlessness and impotence. Just like when my mother Joan and her moods ruled my life, I felt like danger lurked around every corner, like the ground was unsteady beneath my feet.

*Bad things happen, will always happen, have always happened. Bad things especially happen to you.*

Back then, I was young and fierce and fought against giving up and giving in to the power of Joan's violence and venom. I had fought so hard. Now at this different place, I knew what all that fighting got me: just more pain. What really was the point of all the effort then? Why struggle against the rising tide?

I began to obsess again about my dad and the hero of my youth. His kindness and love were the only bright patches in the depths of those memories. The nicknames he gave me and the sound of his truck tires pulling up in the driveway. Reading the paper with him and watching Archie Bunker while cuddling into his lap. Driving for ice cream.

Yes, driving for ice cream. That was the last time I had seen him alive and I played the memory repeatedly in my head like a movie, pausing, rewinding, analyzing. It was a late summer evening and his left hand was holding a cigarette outside the driver's window. I had the taste of raspberry ice cream on my tongue as well as some sass in my mouth, and I had complained about Joan.

"I want you to know that everything is going to be fine now," Dad had said. "Everything is going to be better for you and your sister from now on."

He had looked so serious and sincere, and though he had often said something similar, I wanted to believe him so badly. And then the next day, he was dead. I shook my head to try to remove the image of that evening's newspaper, the photo of my father facedown on the floor with his slippers on and a bloody puddle beneath him. It was burned into my memory, though, permanent.

*Was he simply repeating the same empty reassurances I'd heard dozens -- if not hundreds -- of times? Or this time, did he have a real plan of action? Was that plan the way it turned out in the end, with him dead?*

I thought extensively about the facts I knew about that bloody afternoon. There was a stack of money on the table that no one could explain. Was he trying to bribe her into leaving? Was he threatening her that he was going to leave unless she immediately stopped the abuse? He had left us for a while during the "vacation" separation. Perhaps this time, he would have taken me and Michelle, too.

"Can I have a moment of your time?" That's what Dad apparently asked before the violence went down, according to Joan. What a crazy thing to say and what a formal way to say it. Knowing Dad and his speech patterns, it rang hollow and false. Too much seemed false. Why was he wearing his slippers and not his work boots? He would never have returned from work and exchanged his boots for a pair of slippers. Why was he even home at that time of day?

I could not understand why he had chosen a rifle that day from among the other handful of guns that he owned. It was hardly made for short range use. It was claimed that he fired at her three times, but the only witnessed shot was the third, when our neighbor Mr. Davidson saw my father sighting along the barrel and pulling the trigger. But then how did he shoot himself, twice? Though no expert on weapons, I could see that it was hard enough to turn such a long barreled gun toward one's own chest while keeping a finger on the trigger. Yet he allegedly shot himself in the chest, lowered the gun and turned it around to cock it, and returned it to his chest and shot himself again.

Maybe he had planned on only using the long and awkward weapon to threaten Joan, not planning to actually shoot it. Perhaps there had been a struggle for the gun at some point. Was he already injured when he then shot at Joan? Was it only my belief in Joan's pure evil that made me think she had more to do with the incident than she admitted to the police? Was someone else involved? Most of Joan's life was lived outside of our home after all. She was gone almost every evening to "classes." Did she have a lover? Was he in the house? Was he the shooter? Something was off about it. Something didn't add up.

My eyes cried many tears about it, and my brain couldn't add it up except as a tragedy that took away my father. I had a difficult time wrapping my mind around the choice involved, the choice to take his own life. As I bobbed on the seas of my deep depression, I obsessed over the actual moment that Dad had pulled the trigger and what had made him do it. I suspected he hadn't planned on killing himself that awful day. There was no note – notes are a major sign of planning, as the recent police investigations had made very clear to me. He wasn't a depressive personality, a whiner, or prone to self reflection. I know being married to Joan for decades would try the patience of any man, perhaps eventually driving him to such a desperate act.

I had the suspicion that the end result had at least something to do with Dad's pride. We could never go back to church after our name was listed on the tithing non-payment blackboard. He would never admit he couldn't understand big vocabulary words or do complex math quickly in his head. I don't think he wanted to face the consequences of what he'd done in shooting at Joan -- whether it was planned or in the heat of the moment. He would never have been able to stomach his children visiting him in prison or being shamed by the gossip about a big trial.

Obviously, there was no way of finding out his intentions and, in the end, it really doesn't matter what he'd planned or why he pulled the trigger. Whether he made the decision hours beforehand or if he made an impulsive, split second decision, he'd still done it. He'd raised a gun to his torso, shot himself twice and bled to death while still on the floor of the house. That was what everyone concluded anyway, and I had no evidence to the contrary.

He'd made a choice. He had acted.

And he'd left me alone in the world, adrift among a world full of people who didn't care two shakes about me, some of whom even actively disliked me. He'd been the one bright spot, and the candle had been snuffed out.

My strong and loving father was now in a "better place," or so they said. My Kaela was in that same better place. The place I was living in was pretty downright awful. A better place sounded nice. Anything was better than this pain that refused to relent. Time heals all wounds. I'd heard it said all my life. My wounds were getting worse, and festering, and time didn't appear to be soothing them at all.

I wandered the house like a ghost, sometimes sleeping for more than 12 hours a day with the help of a non-prescription sleep aid. I would emerge only to occasionally grocery shop, when I'd fill up a good portion of the shopping cart with wine.

Philip, on the other hand, continued to commute into the city every morning to oversee our joint government contracting business. He'd carefully shave and dress, then stand in the doorway. I usually hid in the safe cave beneath the covers to avoid his gaze, but he knew I wasn't asleep.

"Come on, Lorijane," he said. "You were handling things. You were working. You were fine. And now this?"

He paused, seeing if I would make any response, then he sighed. His voice was sharp and disapproving.

"Get up and go do something. Stop your sulking already."

Our interactions were growing nastier by the day and I came to hate the sound of his key in the door every evening.

Again, people and places and events out in the world had ceased to matter to me. It was my ever-present thoughts that made up my universe. I thought that the superficial lives that everyone else was leading were more fake than what I was living, what I was going through.

When I wasn't reliving and examining my childhood, I was replaying Kaela's death in the same obsessive way. Like Dad, she was again the person that was closest to me in the universe and her life had ended – abruptly, without warning – and according to some, voluntarily. I still thought that perhaps her and David's plan was originally different, that perhaps they were only going to run away. I knew that even if she'd agreed on the surface at the last moment to such a dramatic and final escape as was provided by a lover's bullet, it was only through his manipulation and coercion. But she, too, had that moment of death, a moment of decision to kneel down voluntarily on the deck in front of David, and I wondered what that moment felt like for her. How is it for anyone who kneels down with the expectation that the one holding the gun will soon be pulling the trigger? I had seen similar scenes depicted in movies and some still war photographs in a magazine or two.

Was it the flipping of some kind of switch, the same exact switch that had clicked for Dad when he was faced with the ultimate reality of his life? Did he suddenly understand that his life was over, that he had just crossed way over the line, and it was time to just end it? Was this propensity or *ability* for suicide hereditary, and if so, was that also my destiny?

Even if it wasn't genetic, there was a common thread between the two death events: *me*. How much value can a person so repeatedly and easily left behind have in this world? If that's the way that even my supposed loved ones treat me, I didn't deserve anything but bad things in my life. Somehow, I had brought this upon myself. My worthlessness was a powerful force, like a black hole, drawing those I love into oblivion. Therefore not only was I worthless, I was also dangerous.

To myself. To others.

I kept thinking about that imaginary, biologically-activated death switch. One little click of a neuron, and the basic and innate human survival instinct went out the window. One click and you had the power over your own life (or end thereof), stealing that power from a world that only wanted to constantly bombard you with more pain and guilt and sadness and stress.

I don't know if suicide is genetic, and neither does the professional psychiatric community. I don't know if that suicide "on-off" switch is implanted in the genes or a product of what happens to you in life; nature or nurture. Especially when considering the cloudy mass of my own family, it could be either. We shared the same genes and the same environment, Dad, Kaela, and I. We were awash in a sea of manipulative people doing harm to our spirits.

As I sat there in the cloistered and stuffy stillness of my empty house -- empty of my youngest daughter, empty of love between me and my husband -- I found it. I saw the trigger switch and found that it was similar to a toothache, impossible to ignore. Painful, but somehow alluring. Though it was big and red and had "danger" signs all around it, I couldn't help but idly touch it and play with it and think about what would happen if I had the courage of my family destiny.

## Chapter Thirteen

Kaela had not been the suicidal type. All the police and investigators and experts had agreed on that point. She was the girl who got great grades, baked cookies for her math class and gave roses to her bus driver. She was outgoing and social and involved both inside and outside school. Unlike teens exhibiting the classic signs of depression, she wasn't losing or gaining weight, isolating herself physically or emotionally, or taking inventory of her life and possessions. At least from the outside, her choice of death seemed to emerge from the clear blue sky.

Dad had not been the suicidal type. He was a typical male, full of humor, bravado and pride. He'd faced hardships in marriage and money problems, but with his quirky smile and perfectly styled hair, he didn't seem to let anything get to him. His death, too, appeared with no forewarning and no explanation.

Both of them seemed to be ready for a "next phase" in life, but neither was ready to end it. Yet they both did, suddenly, without warning, they just laid it down and moved on, or so the authorities had told me.

In the case of my own downward spiral, the reasons for contemplating the quietude of death are evident and obvious. That's not to say anyone need condone my behavior or reactions because they see their causes: I was grief stricken, and I was in a depressed state of mind focused on pain, shame, blame and self-hatred. It's the reason for the choice to die that haunts those left behind, as I know from multiple experiences. *Why?* Suicide and the suicidal mind are a mystery, a dirty little secret, something that we as a society wish to ignore, to cover up and sweep under the rug.

My evident and obvious pain was a mystery even to me as I experienced it, and my thought processes shocked and surprised me. But however much it hurts me to speak of it, I think it's necessary to dive into that deep, dark rabbit hole and throw light on what happens from the inside.

First of all, there's a lot of extra work required simply to live after tragedy. Yes, of course I mean everyday struggles like getting up out of bed in the morning, or even in the early afternoon. It's a struggle to find an appetite for food or, if you can't, to force yourself to chew and swallow what you logically know is necessary for survival . . . which now has far less value than it did before the loss of those things that made life desirable. But there's also a huge pile of unexpected work that piles up around your ankles or on your shoulders, making it even harder not to dive back under the covers or to chew another bite.

Everywhere I looked it seemed there was something to remind me of Kaela. On trips to the grocery store -- which were becoming fewer -- I would see a young mother pushing a cart with her two small daughters. The feeling would wallop me in the gut that this younger woman was me, in happier times. *Why can she have two healthy living daughters? Why has she been allowed to keep them?* Driving past parks and playgrounds, you might think that I'd gaze fondly out at the smiling, playing kids, becoming tender and nostalgic. Instead, I felt a gaping emptiness inside my chest and stretching down into my intestines, an aching hole that threatened to physically tear me apart. I began to dangerously look away from the road to avoid any sight of children or I would drive complicated routes around such obstacles to get where I needed to go.

Therefore, whenever I had gotten up the courage to clean up, dress and get in the car, I would stare out the windshield at the as yet unopened garage door. I'd play with my keys or listen to the radio. I'd take deep breaths, trying to work up the courage to go out into the world and bear those kicks in the gut that seemed to be inevitable. It was easier to go back inside. It seemed like simple self-preservation.

Face to face wasn't the only place where I encountered such pressing resistance to going about the business of living. I learned quickly that every time I turned on the television, danger lurked on very channel. Certainly, the popularity of crime dramas made a lot of programming off limits. Fake blood and fictional murders and staged crime scenes will never again be entertainment for me, not after I looked out my family room window to see my daughter's personal, all too real crime scene, watching the sheet being pulled over her unbreathing face.

Staying away from all those Law & Order and CSI shows was insufficient; no show was 100 percent safe. There were mothers and daughters arguing. Fictional teen characters were constantly falling in love with fictional bad-boy characters. Every show seemed to have at least one episode where there was a funeral that would re-open the tear gates of my own eyes, and I would sob along with their Hollywood-written grief. Movies I'd once loved suddenly became minefields of dangerous subject matter. As unrelated as it may seem, all the daytime TV commercials for colleges, correspondence courses, new career opportunities and even truck-driving school only drove home the point that Kaela was never going to grow up and have a career of any kind. It also reminded me that her mother was too weak to take hers up again, perhaps ever.

Walking around the house: This cabinet was where she'd left me the monkey stuffed animal before she went away for Christmas with her father. That chair was the one she always sat in for family meals, and the box found shoved in the back of the pantry was her favorite cereal, which no one else was going to eat but I couldn't throw away. The sight of the stair banister could call up a memory of the sound of her backpack jingling and her sneakers thudding as she hurried down the stairs for school. In the bathroom lurked the smell of her shampoo and lotion.

Around every corner skulked a ghost of her memory, and as I merely existed, I was forced to chase those ghosts. Or perhaps it was them tormenting and chasing me. Every trivial task was saddled with an extra layer of meaning and emotional struggle. Every tiny little action was work. Hard work. I don't think anyone ever mentions that in condolence cards, where the standard sentiments are "time heals all wounds" and "she's in a better place."

A life deep in the grief of suicide and personal depression is back-breaking, soul-crushing work. And once you get a small taste of that, it's obvious why staying in bed and away from anything but the comfort of your pillow and the oblivion of sleep is so appealing.

The growing burden of that work grew on me as I attempted to drag it around from day to day, and my mind returned over and over again to the streets of downtown Washington D.C., where I'd met so many haggard faces like the one I saw in the mirror. Kaela's research project into homelessness. She'd looked into the various reasons -- or she'd actually constructed the reasons more as "excuses" -- for people who gave up on life and took to the streets. While they came from varied and often previously successful backgrounds, most had suffered some sort of tragedy, such as death, divorce, mental illness or crime.

So why weren't all people who suffered such common tragedies homeless? Kaela had come to the conclusion that these hapless street people had made a choice, had chosen not to do the hard work of living in the workaday world and confronting and overcoming their own demons. They couldn't muster up the strength or energy to re-enter the fray of battle.

I had applauded Kaela's precociousness and prescience when she came to such mature (I had once thought) and well thought out conclusions. But with all that had happened to me and with the choices that Kaela had eventually made despite her previous insights, I was on a different side of the equation. I was on the side of the poor souls who threw up their hands and gave up fighting with the world. I was on Kaela's side of things. I understood that there was no point in fighting, that surrender was the only sane option. At that point, it seemed my only option. I now understood how Dad had felt in that final moment of realization.

I thought intensely about the suicide switch in my brain, and I felt like the character Snagglepuss on the Hanna Barbera cartoons of my childhood. Every time things got complicated or he was about to be in trouble, he'd hitch up his elbows and say, "Exit, stage left!" as he disappeared into a cloud of motion blur.

I'd gone to church most of my life. I never robbed a bank or stole from anyone, and I certainly never killed or physically injured anyone. I'd never done anything seriously wrong. *So why are you doing this to me, God? I have tried to be a good person. Why?* I questioned God and the point of existence and my daughter and my family and my pathetic nature and my stupid tears and my painful emotions. It came down to the thought, *I'm not supposed to be here. I can't be here.*

I just wanted to go away. To disappear. To exit, stage left . . . .

*

I admitted it aloud in my head. I wanted to die. I was willing to kill myself. The thought wasn't *I'm going to kill myself* or *I will kill myself now.* But I didn't stand there with my finger on the switch and admit to myself that I really, desperately wanted to pull the trigger.

At first no one knew, or at least, I made it a point to believe that no one knew. It's not like when you walk into a grocery store, there's a big, flashing sign above your head that says, "Hello, I'm severely depressed and suicidal." There are no code words that suicidal people alone say, or if there are, I wasn't speaking them to anyone who could discern what was going on inside of me. That was kind of thrilling in a way, like being a spy in the camp of the normal people and being very good at sneaking around in disguise, dressed like one of them.

It was more of an effort with family and friends, however, but I did continue to use the mask I'd begun constructing when Kaela first died. I'd force a smile, even if it was a sad or bittersweet one. I'd talk about the weather or about their own lives, trying to seem as if I had an interest in the outside world. I'd talk about how I thought I was turning a corner or that I was considering going back to work. Soon, but not yet.

But in the privacy of aloneness, closed off from the suburban world outside my door by fancy window curtains and thick walls, I started to imagine and plan.

It perhaps started with pills. I had been retreating into the world of sleep with the help of a few glasses of wine and four or five non-prescription sleeping pills every night for weeks, if not months. But one night, I paused with the bottle open. I poured out four, but then I shook out a few more. They were so placid and blue and inviting, so smooth and clean. I poured out even more until my whole cupped hand was full. Then I looked in the bottle to see how many more were left. Plenty. Enough.

I had been sitting on the bed with one foot beneath me, but I stood up and went to the bathroom. With the full hand protectively held out to the side, I filled up a glass of water, all the way to the top. I stopped for a moment to consider myself in the mirror. I was still disheveled, but I looked somehow more pulled together. I confidently met my own eye and stood tall. I looked over at the hand filled with pills through the reflection of the mirror, and I thought a little longer.

I took a sip of my water and brought the glass back to the bedside table. I stared at the blue pills for a few more moments before I shoveled all but four of them back into the bottle and screwed on the cap. I took those four with some more water, and as I lay down to wait for the comforting release of sleep, I thought about the surety, calmness and power I'd just felt as I stood in the bathroom contemplating my death. It had felt rather good.

*I need to think about this a little more,* I thought. *I really need to think about this.*

Starting the next morning, I did actively think about suicide and methods of committing suicide. So like any modern woman, I sat down at the computer and went to the Internet to research and to answer some of my many questions, questions that had been under the surface for some time but which now were bobbing up freely in the light of day.

I started looking up information about the pills. The Internet is a wealth of knowledge about anything medical, and this subject was no different. I found out about which pain killers would do the job, and how much would be dangerous or fatal to people of different weights. It was framed as precautionary information instead of a "how-to" manual, but it served my purposes nonetheless. I found out the stages of death and that it was usually a peaceful way to go. That sounded rather nice, I thought.

However, it was common for those poisoning themselves with painkillers to vomit, either while they were still conscious (that wouldn't be too peaceful) or while they were unconscious. Either way, whoever found the body wouldn't be confronted by what looked to be a peacefully sleeping loved one. Instead, the face turned blue and dried vomit would cake their lips, cheeks and nearby bedding. That seemed disgusting and repulsive and not exactly the last vision of me I wanted my family to remember. It just wasn't . . . tidy. Vain as that sounds, it was of significant consideration to me. Plus, there would be an intolerable mess, and smell -- intolerable at least to my nature -- that was hard for my clean-obsessed psyche to come to grips with.

I didn't like guns at all, and in fact, I didn't own one, so that seemed out of the question. Having thought over and over about how my father had used that long rifle to awkwardly shoot himself -- not once, but twice -- I knew that guns were far from an easy way out. They were not guaranteed in anyone's hands, but were especially risky in mine. I had been in the military, but I wasn't an expert or a good marksman by any means.

In addition, I had seen the pool of blood Dad had died in. I had helped clean it up. I had seen the pool of blood my daughter had died in. Guns were messy and my fastidious, obsessively tidy nature did not want to create such a mess, even if I would not have to deal with the aftermath personally. I may be dead, but my house and my world would have that massive stain. I couldn't stand the thought of the stain itself or who would be forced to deal with it. Philip? Niki? I crossed the firearm option off my mental list.

Death by hanging? It could be fast if the neck snapped. If not, suffocation would cause the head to turn blue and swell. Vomit was also possible. Slitting the wrists? Would I be buried with bandages on my wrists, or with big, open gashes? How would I contain all that blood?

Then I got more dramatic. I thought about getting in my Jaguar, which after all was meant to handle high speeds and tight turns, and I would drive up into the hills to someplace very remote. I didn't know exactly where, but the kind of road that had guardrails to hold the cars against a high precipice and with very few streetlights; very shadowed. I could simply close my eyes and accelerate into a curve without turning the wheel, flying out into space. I could kill myself without hurting anyone but me.

But what if I didn't die on impact, and instead cost my family months of ICU visits and orthopedic therapy to save a life I didn't want? Maybe I should carry some gasoline with me in the car. Would it ignite? The thought of my skin roasting off my bones was repugnant. Being cooked to death wasn't really a simple, painless and clean way to go at all.

I spent most of my days minutely planning different scenarios of suicide, but now really, actively planning -- like someone packing and re-packing for an upcoming vacation. I spent hours making an inventory of everything that belonged to me in the house, in the garage and in other storage. Then I split it up in different ways, deciding who of my family and friends or what charity should be the beneficiary of each item. I wrote up several versions of my will.

I also crafted dozens of versions of my suicide note, and mine was going to be everything that Kaela's had not been. Some drafts were short and to the point, others were long missives with messages to everyone and instructions on my funeral arrangements. All of them, however, were dripping with pain, agony and depression.

I didn't want to go on. I would rather feel nothing than what I had to experience every day. I felt like this was the only choice I could make. I wanted my note to make no bones about that fact, to leave none of the doubt I felt about Kaela's unclear note or Dad's lack of one.

I struggled the most with the apologetic sentiments that most suicide notes included, the sorrys you say to those you leave behind. If I was sure of what I wanted to do, how do you apologize at the same time? I was sorry to be leaving in some ways -- mainly to leave my daughter Niki, whom I loved deeply, even though she was still a wild child -- but I was not sorry to fade into the blackness. It would be a welcome relief, like a balm on severely burned skin. I couldn't phrase the right words, even if I did still have feelings of being sorry for leaving behind emotional pain for others.

I carefully destroyed and disposed of each one in their turn after whatever suicidal act in my head didn't pan out, when I didn't have the guts. But I continued to toe closer and closer to the line, until one day, I did.

In the middle of the night, I crept from our bedroom down the stairs to the main-level garage. I was dressed in my pajamas and carried a few pairs of old, worn socks, and I picked up the keys to one of the cars from the hallway desk. I couldn't help but pause and run my fingers over the place where Kaela had taped up her final note to the living world. It felt like there should have been some mark still remaining -- a groove, a stickiness, something -- but it was unscarred and smooth. The scar on my heart, however, throbbed with renewed grief. Because it's constantly there, itching under your skin, you never know it's abated slightly until it swells to full strength again. Or perhaps it never abates. We only grow used to the pain until it again increases.

I stepped out to our garage in my socked feet, trying to silently close the heavy door. Then I stuffed a few pairs of socks into the tailpipe of the car and slid into the driver's seat. I don't remember if I had a note that particular first time, for it would turn out that I often came down around three a.m. to sit in the same seat and contemplate the same thing while I nervously ran my hands along the steering wheel. If I did have one, I would have it with me.

Then I would place the key in the ignition and start the engine.

In the closed garage and with the closed tailpipe, I wondered how long it would take, often consulting my watch. My eyes stared unfocused through the glass of the windshield, thinking about the nothingness of the middle distance and what relief it would offer. I touched my face -- often wiping away my tears -- and I stroked the smooth leather of the seats in agitation, thinking that soon the physical world would go away, that I would no longer be able to feel through these fingertips as well as see through these eyes, live with these memories or carry around this pain.

What most people would not understand is that these thoughts made me feel free and powerful, able to literally float away beyond the flesh-and-blood world of pain and loss. It was like a superpower of a sort. I would breathe heavily out through my mouth and very consciously take in air through my nose, tasting and savoring the smell of my oncoming death in the form of poisonous carbon-monoxide gases. I made breathing active and forceful.

*I am doing this. I am doing something. I am leaving.*

I would begin to feel the gases' effects on my body. I felt heavy and tired. My eyes were dry, itchy and the vision was somewhat pulled and distorted. My head spun. Eventually, I began to feel nauseous. I thought I might throw up.

I began to think about the disgusting nature of vomit and how what little I had for dinner would be on display for the world and for family history to chronicle. I thought about corrosive stomach acid eating away at the upholstery of the car, which I had always lovingly maintained. I thought about the vomit crusting on my cheeks and in my hair and on my lap, and the thought revolted me to the core. I wished I had latex gloves and disinfectant and paper towels on hand. My skin itched with the idea of the nastiness of the color, texture and smell of vomit, and my psyche cried out that it could not, would not, do such a thing.

And that's the point at which I usually reached out with a shaking hand to turn the key back to the off position.

I took a few shuttering breaths. The garage was still thick with poisonous gases, and my symptoms didn't immediately begin to disappear. I sat there confused, not knowing whether I should relish the symptoms and the feeling of freedom and power they had created, or immediately flee from what I had almost done. My mind was torn. Half wanted me to stop being such a coward and turn the key again, to finish what I had started. The other half still itched and revolted against the idea.

In the end, I made sure all the gas had dissipated and crept back through the garage door to the house, making sure that I didn't smell of the exhaust when I returned to bed. Until I crept down the next time to repeat the exercise all over again. After such an attempt, I always went to sleep with dreams of wings and clouds and other free-floating imagery, or I dreamed of blackness, dreaming nothing. Both were an intense relief until I woke up the next morning to see that nothing had really changed and that I must face the crushing work of living another day yet again.

I arose and went through the motions, telling people what they wanted to hear to keep them off my back. I didn't want more cards or flowers or offers of companionship. I literally wanted nothing, but I kept the idea of suicide in my back pocket, like a thug hides his secret switchblade.

One night a couple of well-meaning, supportive and wonderful friends managed to get me out of the house to go out for a fun and frivolous dinner. They chose something bright and somewhat silly to try to raise my spirits, and so I found myself nibbling on a shared order of hot wings and sipping on a drink in a local Hooters restaurant. It was full summer outside, mid July, six months after Kaela's death, and I was wearing a sundress in an attempt to play along with their good will and high spirits.

My friends tried to draw me out with small talk and conversation about Niki, and I answered as much as I could bear, diverting the topic into the events of their own lives. But I found that my friends still carefully and lovingly prodded me, which took me by surprise. During the tragic periods of my childhood and Dad's suicide, every person's reaction was to brush the incident under the rug and pretend it didn't exist. Only the weak or the traitorous would openly confront the event or share their reactions to it. But decades later in the culture of the 21st Century, it was okay to feel pain and talk about your feelings. It was, in fact, encouraged, and my friends tried to let me know that they could be a safe audience for me.

I couldn't do it, however. I couldn't talk about the raging and thunderous mess that was going on inside my head. It was too shameful and embarrassing, and I knew what they would say anyway: that it wasn't my fault, that time heals all wounds, *et cetera*. That wasn't going to help, because they didn't understand. And if they did understand, surely they would be shocked and repulsed by the awful person I really was. I said monosyllables to placate, simultaneously feeling I was an even worse person for treating good people that way, for shutting them out when they only wanted to help. It only confirmed my worthlessness.

Still, I hoped I was fooling them with the act, because if they knew what was going on in my head, they were going to make me live, make me continue hurting.

I excused myself from the table, grabbing the belted cardigan I'd brought to throw on when the summer night grew chilly. I headed to the restroom, where I could get away from the people -- my friends, but still encroaching people -- who felt like a flock of birds beating their wings about my head. I needed some silence and solitude, and I stood in the locked stall for some time, trying to make sense of my thoughts.

*Why did I come here -- come out with them? Why didn't I just stay home? Why didn't I just . . .*

My eyes caught on to the hook on the back of the stall door, meant to hold your coat or purse. I looped a finger around it and pulled. It felt like it could hold more than that. Without much more thought, I removed the belt of my cardigan from its loops and stretched the material out to check for give and strength. It was woven strong and tight. I looked again at the hook.

*It's worth a try. It would be better than you feel now.*

I looped the sweater around my neck and tightened it. Then using a knot that I'd learned about in my hours of suicide research, I prepared a loop to go around the hook, which was inches higher off the ground than I was tall. I stood up on my tiptoes and looped the belt around the hook, pulling it tight so I couldn't get it untied in a panic.

And I let my legs go limp.

There was an immediate change of pressure in my head, as if I had instantly dropped to 100 feet beneath the ocean. My eyes felt like they were bulging, and sparks appeared at the corners of my vision. My head grew burning hot. The belt bit in tighter than I could ever have imagined, and I felt very close to death. I felt like I could reach out and part a curtain to meet death face-to-face. My body was getting more distant.

And then I backed out. My arm was heavy and clumsy as I flung it above my head, groping for the belt. I fumbled at the knot I'd so recently wanted not to give way under any circumstances and prayed it would untie. After a few seconds that seemed like minutes, grimacing, I was able to loosen it enough to wrench my head from its loop, straining my neck at impossible angles.

I stood on the formica tile of the stall and gasped, breathing hard. I doubled over in an attempt get more air -- just as someone else entered the restaurant bathroom.

"Are you okay?" she shouted, panicked and loud. She couldn't help but hear the loud, labored and ragged breathing. Her footsteps quickened up to the door of my stall.

"Yes," I croaked, then cleared my throat and managed a more normal tone. "I'm just getting sick. It will pass."

"Are you sure?" Even the shoes under the door seemed reticent to believe me.

"Yeah, I just need to sit for a moment. Could you tell me friends I'll be right out?" I asked, telling her at which table they were sitting. I took a moment to compose myself, left the stall and splashed cold water on my face.

I didn't really know how to feel. I felt better for some reason, knowing there was an escape route out of the emotional space I was in. I felt proud because I knew that secret and that I came so close, me of all people. And I felt ashamed at myself, because I knew that these positive emotions about attempting suicide were wrong, that there was something wrong with me for feeling elated about something like this.

It all feeds into the loop of depression. I am an awful, hurting person, and I therefore want to leave this world. But only awful people leave the world in such a way --

let alone look forward to it or feel prideful about it -- so I am even more disgusting and deplorable.

*But I hadn't gotten caught. No one knew.*

*

Like most untreated mental disorders, lack of treatment caused my disorder to grow bigger, bolder and stronger. The endorphins that released when I touched that switch of life and death became more alluring and addictive, to the point that I knew one of these times, I was actually going to let the switch hit home. I was going to turn the lights off. It was only a question of when.

Suicide was in my genes. I killed the people that I loved. I was destined to die and I deserved to die. The strength of those convictions and the strength I felt because I knew I was capable of the powerful act combined to make me bold.

Of course, my condition was more obvious to the people around me than I thought at the time, but in the month of July, it became impossible to ignore.

One night at around3:30 in the morning, I was sitting in the running car, my eyes half shut and breathing as if in a meditative state, which I suppose I sort of was. I didn't hear the door open, but I did hear the sudden banging of Philip's knuckle against the glass of the driver's window.

"What in the hell do you think you're doing?" he demanded. His eyes were sparking with rage.

I shook my head to clear it and stopped the car's engine. "I must have fallen asleep," I replied, faking a yawn. "I just needed to get out of here." I was totally improvising. "I felt like I need to go somewhere."

His lips compressed into an angry line and he opened the door of the car. He took my arm, and led me toward the house in a way that was more dragging than escorting.

"Next time you want to go somewhere, start by opening the garage," he growled, as he did just that, letting all the exhaust drain out into the night.

I don't think he completely believed my story. It's possible he thought I had been drinking too much wine, which I probably had been in addition. I do know that he didn't want to admit to himself what had been going on, what I was going through. If he did, it was one more thing he had to deal with and he wanted to have as little to do with me as possible since I began to crumble. It was easier to look away in denial.

On the weekends, Philip tried to keep the facade of normality by driving out us out to the marina to spend some time in the sun on our boat. It was the same boat where we entertained Kaela and Niki and their friends, which had been a good part of the fun of it for me. Alone with Philip, I felt like an empty nester, but an empty nester stuck with a rotting egg. I saw Kaela sunning herself on the deck, comparing her olive-tan skin with mine. I saw her laughing. I remembered how I thought a summer on the water and having fun would distract her from David. In truth, David had permanently distracted her from any life and any future fun. It was a memory prison on the waves.

On more than one occasion, I got out of control on the dock, drinking too much either on deck or in the marina bar. I picked fights with Philip and with people who came up trying to offer condolences I didn't want.

One afternoon on the boat, I flew into a rage and told Philip I was going to kill myself. I locked myself in the bathroom with a steak knife. I was so desperate for relief that the itching of skin thinking about bloody messes and unhealed, dead wounds on my wrists didn't matter. I overcame it, and I pressed the steak knife into the flesh of my wrist and pulled. The knife was dull. The wound hurt, but it was only a shallow, ragged line on my skin. It would heal within days.

*I can't even manage that,* I thought in despair.

I was forced to reappear on deck and tell Philip that I was being overemotional, that I didn't really mean it. I don't know if he saw the wound despite my attempt to hide it.

The declarations started to come more often.

"You need to get out, Lorijane. Go to the grocery store, maybe. There's no food in the house. You need to eat something," he said, standing in the kitchen.

"What do you care?" I asked. "By next week, I'll be dead anyway."

He brought his hand down on the counter top. "Now stop it, Lorijane," he shouted. "You're just asking for attention with all of this. Snap out of it now. Jesus."

Niki would come over to visit me whenever she could. She had her own life, and even though she was out on her own, she got into teenage trouble and was busy doing things I wouldn't approve of. Even so, she was the one person in the world I would see and talk to every time she came. She started to become more and more upset as the summer passed.

"Mom," she said. "When was the last time you took a shower?"

"Oh, I did a few days ago," I said, waving her away. I thought that answer was perfectly acceptable.

"And you're not eating."

"You don't know that. You're not here."

"What are you eating? What did you eat today?"

I was silent, thinking. I couldn't pull up the memory of the last time I had food through the hurricane of memory and emotion that had thoroughly taken over my brain.

"Mom." She grabbed my shoulder and maneuvered me into the bathroom and in front of the large mirror. "Look at yourself."

I saw a worthless person with bags under her sad eyes. I didn't see anyone of value. *Who cares? What does it matter?*

"Look at this," she commanded, and pulled up the hem of my shirt to reveal pants that I had safety pinned to fit my shrinking waist. I had been about 130 pounds when Kaela died, and I got down to about 95 pounds in the depths of my depression. "You're wasting away."

I met her eyes in the mirror, and she dropped my shirt. Her expression was equally worried and angry at the situation, that the state of affairs were this bad. These were serious problems from her viewpoint.

"What do you want me to do?" I asked. "I don't know what you want me to do!"

I dissolved into tears and she gave me a hug, engulfing me because I had become so small.

"We're going to fix this," she said.

I don't know if she and Philip spoke, but directly after Niki confronted me, he did, too. He walked up to where I was sitting on the couch with the home laptop open in his hand.

"What are you doing here?" he asked, pulling up the search history and pointing to the screen. I tried not to look, but I already knew the phrases I had put there. There was no way to wiggle out of what I had been looking for. He obviously already knew the type of research I had been doing.

Then he pulled a few fragments of paper out of his pocket. "And what are you doing here?" he asked. He handed them to me, and I recognized my handwriting and the paper as one of the suicide notes I had drafted and left behind, torn up in the waste basket.

"This is it, Lorijane. No more," he said. "You are going to have to get help. Now. No more pretending things are okay one moment and doing things like this when no one's looking. You need help."

He moved to force me to make eye contact with him.

"This is an ultimatum. You will get help. Do you understand?"

Tears were leaking out from my eyes and burning down my face. I knew if I attempted words, all that would emerge would be a sob, and so I nodded. I just nodded.

## Chapter Fourteen

Just because you're miserable doesn't mean that you look forward to getting help, as I soon found out. Philip had given me an ultimatum that I needed to find someone to help me with my grief, depression and suicidal thoughts, but I had to force myself to act on the demand. I was scared of opening myself up to a psychiatrist or counselor; scared that they wouldn't be able to help me, and scared that perhaps they would. Change is difficult to process, even if you're changing from a *status quo* of feeling horrible.

I had no method of choosing one doctor or clinic over another one. I just opened up the phone book to their listings for mental health providers, closed my eyes and stabbed one listing with my finger, choosing blind. The clinic's logo was a cartoon of a person's head with the top hinged open, with all these little squiggles and symbols exploding out into the air. I thought it was silly, but I nonetheless called up their office and made an appointment.

It was strange how very normal it all felt when I arrived. The clinic was located in a quiet office park, average and unremarkable. The grass was tidy and the sidewalks swept. I walked through the door into a waiting room that could have been any doctor's office, complete with well-thumbed magazines and a few potted plants. The receptionist was polite and smiled sweetly when she gave me a clipboard of paperwork to fill out, and everyone else in the waiting room seemed utterly normal.

I don't know what I was expecting. Something crazier, I guess, given that this is where people came when they started slipping into the crazy category. Perhaps the other people in the waiting room were more nervous than other strangers you see, maybe a little redder around the eyes, but they looked like the same people I saw at the grocery store or in the car in the lane next to mine or out walking dogs along the street. Just average folks. Part of me was intensely relieved, and part of me just felt more nervous. Were they looking at me for signs of disturbance, too? Was there a tattoo on my forehead that read "suicidal" for everyone could see? I shifted in my chair anxiously until my name was called.

I stood up to confront my new doctor.

"Hi, Lorijane," he said, extending his hand to me. "I'm Dr. Nelson." He shook my hand warmly and firmly, obviously making an effort to be as welcoming as possible. He was young -- much younger than I expected -- and quite handsome in a boyish way, with short brown hair, brown eyes and a stylish, colorful tie. He led me down a hallway lined with doors on both sides. Outside each door was what I came to find out was a white noise machine, which guaranteed the privacy of the patient inside and made them feel more comfortable in divulging very personal information and emotions.

Dr. Nelson opened the door of his office for me, gestured me inside and then closed it softly behind him. I found myself in a quiet room furnished with bookshelves, a large desk, several chairs and a couch, which I assumed is where I was supposed to sit. I perched on the end of the cushion, chin up and shoulders back as the doctor pulled one of the chairs up near the couch and sat, a note pad balanced on his crossed legs.

"So," he began, making eye contact with me. "How are you today?"

I almost laughed. *I mean, would anybody be in a place like this if they were feeling well?*

"I'm managing, I suppose," I answered. "I got here."

He nodded. "So it was a bit of a struggle for you to come in here, to ask for help?"

"I didn't really have a choice. My husband and my daughter kind of demanded that I get help of some sort, and so . . ." I threw my hands up. "Here I am."

"Have you ever been in therapy before?"

"Once," I said. "After my daughter was born. Some postpartum depression issues."

"Well, let me tell you a little bit about how I work here so you can get comfortable and know what to expect. Obviously the first thing you need to know is that this is a safe place. Nothing we talk about here will ever go beyond these walls, unless it seems that you are a danger to yourself or others. The law requires that of me. I understand from when you made the appointment that you're seeking grief therapy, so that's where we can start. Mostly just through talk therapy, but we can talk about medication as the need arises, too."

"I don't want any medication," I interjected. I had been taking too much medication already. My body felt weak and ill, the after-effects of living on little food and lots of sleep and pain meds swallowed with substantial doses of wine. I felt heavy and tender, and I didn't want to add often controversial depression medication to the cocktail, at least not if I could help it. In fact, I had decided that I wanted to get through this on my own two feet, having a hunch that was the only way it was going to stick. Hospitals and medications were crutches I didn't want to lean on. Perhaps none of these rationales was true -- maybe I had no intention of getting through it at all.

He nodded, seeming to accept this.

"Also, I always mention this to new clients, because it seems to be something most of them consider." He cracked a smile. "I know I'm rather young. However, I assure you that I'm highly qualified and dedicated, and that if I ever believe that my inexperience is hindering the quality of care I provide, I can always turn to other members of our team. I want you to feel that I'm open and honest and that you can trust me."

I swallowed, sensing that it would soon be my turn to speak and feeling tears beginning to well in my eyes. But I genuinely appreciated his honesty in tackling the subject of his age. It soothed me and made me feel that he was a genuine and upfront person.

"So, why don't you tell me a little bit about yourself and what brings you in here today?"

I bit my lip. "Well," I said. "My daughter, Kaela. She . . . she died, in January. Her boyfriend shot her and I saw her die on my back deck."

My voice was cracking and uneven, but I continued to talk, letting it all stream from me. I don't know how much sense it made that first time I told Dr. Nelson the story of my life, because I wasn't really able to keep in chronological. I told him about how I introduced Kaela to David, about her sneaking around and lying about their relationship. I talked about Niki and her ADD and acting out. Then I jumped into my abandonment by my family and my time in foster care, then jumped back to the blame I suffered after Kaela's death. I talked about Philip and how I was increasingly feeling threatened by him, emotionally and physically. Eventually, I told him very briefly about my parents' shooting and how I worried the past and the present were linked. Then I had to tell him about the back deck, about the bloody vision on the back deck that I felt would haunt me for the rest of my life.

And of course, I told him I was miserable.

"I just don't want to do it anymore. I don't want to be here anymore," I said, sniffing. "I just . . . don't know what to do." I knew I had to tread lightly there, remembering how he had just said something about him being forced by law to act if he believed me to be *a danger to myself or others*. "I'm so used to just not talking about any of this stuff, this emotional stuff. It's like when I was a kid, they taught me to think that what happened to my dad or anything private was a secret, that the strong thing to do was bottle it up. It was shameful not to," I continued. "Talking to you, like this . . . it seems weird."

"I understand," said Dr. Nelson, who throughout my story had remained calm and connected. "A lot of families react that way to tragedy, and it might take you some time to become accustomed to being so open. But I have to say, I think that your story is truly tragic and I'm glad that you've decided to reach out for help and to reach out to me. It's a fascinating case from a medical perspective, and I'll say right now, grief on this scope is something I've not dealt with before in depth, but it's a challenge that I want to confront along with you. Though it's likely to be a long road back to you feeling strong and well again, I'm glad that I can help you along that path."

Dr. Nelson seemed so sincere, so kind. I wanted to believe him and to trust him, to open up the top of my head like the clinic's logo and spill out the mess for him to fix up as good as new. But I couldn't. I physically couldn't push the words out of my mouth to talk about the ragged steak knife cut on my arms, being pulled from the running car by Philip, the feeling of power I got holding too many pills or the incident in the ladies' room where I'd almost seen the other side of the thin veil between this world and the next. So I shut my mouth and bottled that away, just like I'd always been taught.

I looked into his kind face, and I wondered if he knew what he was getting himself into.

*

We began meeting three times a week for several hours each session, and I began to think about the meetings as a sort of dance. Dr. Nelson and I would carefully step around one another, he'd parry forward and I'd retreat back, he'd step up again to lure me out. He wanted to know things about me that I didn't talk to anyone about, that I didn't even bring up with myself. My intimate thoughts, my sex life, my spiritual beliefs. I tried to be as honest as possible without telling the whole truth in an attempt at what I thought was self preservation, but was really only the continuation of a cycle of self destruction.

"So you have thought about suicide yourself then?" he asked point blank, probing right to the heart of the issue. "Obviously with what you've been through, that wouldn't be uncommon."

I nodded.

"Can you elaborate on that?"

"I get frustrated, especially after Kaela's death, with how no one can even hope to understand. They say the stupidest things that just make you feel worse. Like, 'She's in a better place now.' They said that about my Dad, too. So what's this better place then? Where is it? Why do they get to be there and not me? It sometimes seems like they were the smart ones, leaving all this behind once and for all."

Dr. Nelson’s lips were pressed together, turned down at the edges. He was quiet for a moment.

"You know," I said, trying to shift away from the dangerous subject, "your left shoe needs to be resoled. It's coming apart at the heel there."

His eyebrows arched up in surprise and he tilted his shoe up to get a look at the underside. "Well, look at that," he said. "What made you take notice of that?"

"It's the kind of thing I notice," I said. I paused, trying to put my obsessiveness into words that someone besides myself could understand. "As long as I can remember, I've always liked things very neat, everything in its place. It gets under my skin otherwise, and I can't relax until I fix it or clean it or move it. You've worn those shoes a few times now, and it's been bothering me to no end."

"I see. Anything else bothering you in the office?"

I told him about how the air conditioner vent had a crooked piece of metal, that his books weren't organized by any method that I could see, that there were patches of dust where he or the cleaning crew regularly failed to clean, plus the window glass was smeary. He seemed amused and questioned me further, asking if I had any other rituals.

"Do you wash your hands more often than most people? Do you often have to go back and check to see if you did something, like lock a door?"

"I thought everyone did stuff like that." I told him that yes, I always checked locks repeatedly. I turned on and off light switches in odd numbers -- flicking it three or five times -- because that way I knew it was really on or off. I could spend up to 45 minutes properly making my bed, with every fold and tuck in its proper place.

I'd always known I was a neat freak and I'd idly tossed around the word compulsive to describe myself, but Dr. Nelson confirmed it once and for all. I suffered from a mild case of obsessive compulsive disorder, nothing serious enough to prevent me from leading a normal life but something that nonetheless drove almost all my behavior.

"OCD is usually a coping mechanism, a way of dealing with reality and taming it. It's a way of asserting control over an unruly world," he explained. "Does that feel true to you?"

I nodded, saying that cleaning up and what he called rituals certainly did make me feel safer, more in charge of my life. And then without stopping to censor my thoughts, I found myself talking about how I think that mild OCD might be the only reason why I was there, sitting in front of him, still breathing.

"I think that's probably why I haven't committed suicide," I said. "I think of all these ways of killing myself, but each and every one of them is so dirty, would cause such a mess. If I shot myself, there would be brains on the wall. Overdosing causes vomiting. And of course there's blood. What a mess!"

I smiled with dark humor. Dr. Nelson wasn't smiling.

"So you've actively thought about going through with any or all of those methods of suicide?" he asked. "How recently have you had such thoughts?"

Again, I laughed a little in my dark mood. "What time is it now?" I joked.

I saw the serious look on his face and bit my lip. In a voice that he was obviously trying to keep calm and non-confrontational, Dr. Nelson asked me, "Have you ever taken steps toward such a death, Lorijane? Have you tried to kill yourself?"

I was staring at my lap. For so long -- months -- I had been cowering within my own body, wearing my physical face like a mask and hiding all of these dark thoughts and emotions. It's like I was curled into the fetal position in my own mind, curled around my pain. My pain and I had become very close. Now, it was as if Dr. Nelson had knocked on the door to that private cell and tried to rouse me, to lure me out, to make me show him the tightly held pain I hugged to myself, and it was frightening.

No one knew that weak, hated-filled version of Lorijane. I didn't want anyone to know her lest they hate her the same way I did. *If I tell him the truth,* I wondered, *what will he think of me?*

"Lorijane?" he asked. "Have you ever actually attempted suicide?"

I looked up and met his eyes. I nodded. Suddenly I was talking about the late-night incidents in the garage when I'd left the car running long enough to make my head feel fuzzy, to feel consciousness pulling away. I told him about all the suicide notes I'd composed and then discarded. I felt like I was airing my darkest secrets and the shame made my face hot, but I continued telling him some of the many stories of ways I had almost -- but not quite -- followed through on the attempt to end my life. I found myself talking almost in a trance as I told him how it felt in the restaurant restroom, the extreme lightness and freedom I felt when the oxygen in my head began to run low. He asked a few questions to prod me on, but basically let my thoughts flow out.

The two-hour session was beginning to wind toward its close and I looked at Dr. Nelson almost shyly, wondering if I had done the right thing in opening up the door to my deep, dark subconscious, even if only a crack.

"So how often do you have these suicidal thoughts?" he asked.

"All the time," I whispered, like a child admitting she was afraid of the dark.

"Okay," he sighed. "I'm glad that you're beginning to share with me, but I think I have to tell you that professional guidelines and the law dictate that I must act, that I'm going to have to call the hospital and find a bed for you -- "

"No!" Just like that, the door to my subconscious slammed shut and my mask was again firmly in place. "No," I repeated.

"But Lorijane, you are a danger to yourself."

I laughed. "I'm a danger to myself fifteen times a day," I said. "It's all I think about, about joining my loved ones wherever they may be. Still, I come to your office. Even so, I honestly believe that there's nothing left for me here, don't you understand? No one can understand. No one knows what it's like in here, in this life. It's practically inevitable."

"No, it's not, and I can help you," he assured me.

"Not by committing me. I will not go."

"I have to."

"Then I have to leave," I said. I grabbed my purse and headed for the door.

"I can't let you do that."

"Well, I'm not going to sit here and wonder whether from one moment to the next you're going to change from my helpful doctor to my worst enemy. How can I be here and talk to you if I'm afraid to tell you the truth?"

He explained further his obligation as a therapist, and that his power to commit me was legally enforceable.

"But how are you going to help me if I never come back? I'm standing here right in front of you. The fact that I'm here at all! You can see that I'm not doing anything."

"But how do I know you're not going to do it when you leave?"

"Because I said so."

"But you tell me you keep trying," he protested.

This was going nowhere, I could see, and I wasn't going to budge on the issue.

He looked with pleading eyes, trying to make me understand his position. "I can't in good faith let you drive home."

I stormed out of the room and down the hall, past the white-noise machines and the closed doors, and past the reception desk. I heard him call at least once more, but I didn't even cast a glance back. I headed toward my car: my bright blue Jaguar. While there were a handful of Jaguars in the affluent neighborhood, it was still a pretty obvious vehicle and I needed to think about where I was going, in case he made good on his threat to call the authorities.

I knew I couldn't go home, so I picked up my cell phone and called our regular dog walker. As it rang, another call chimed in and the caller ID said it was Dr. Nelson. I clicked "ignore." The neighborhood dog walker answered the phone, and I asked her if she could please swing by the house this afternoon to take care of the dog as I was going to be unexpectedly away. Then I took off in my Jaguar, trying to think of a place to lie low for a while and get my thoughts in order.

If Dr. Nelson was telling me the truth, he could call the police and have them start looking for my license plate number. Where would a bright blue Jaguar not be so obvious? *Well, in a place where there's lots of other Jaguars.* The good doctor continued to call, and I continued to ignore him.

I was just pulling up to the Jaguar dealership about 20 minutes later when the dog walker called me back.

"Hey, Lorijane," she said. "Is there any reason why you have a police car outside your house? Anything I should be worried about here?"

"No, nothing I'm aware of. I'm sure they have some reason to be in the neighborhood, but I doubt it has anything to do with me. Or the dog." I tried to laugh a little. "Thanks for letting me know, though."

I pulled the car into the back lot of the dealership, where they kept the majority of their inventory but not where they usually took customers. Somehow, no one noticed that once I drove in, I didn't leave the car. Instead, I hunkered down to wait it out a bit.

*What am I doing? What have I done? Why am I doing this? What is wrong with me?*

It gradually got dark as I sat in that metal box and brooded, thoughts whirling. I didn't know why I'd exploded, or why I'd opened up in the first place. Why had I told him all that? It's as if he was the first person to reach me in a long time, to reach down into the black hole I felt I was in, to touch the real Lorijane hiding inside, the honest Lorijane. And it scared me that he'd breached my defenses. The whole therapeutic process was making me feel very vulnerable.

I sat in that parking lot for almost 24 hours, my only company the quickly depleting cell phone that Dr. Nelson continued to call. He was obviously a persistent man. With one bar of battery life yet, I finally made the decision to call him back.

He answered almost immediately, his relief palpable in his voice.

"If I'm going to come back to therapy, I need you to promise me something. I need you to promise that you won't try to hospitalize or medicate me."

"I can't promise that," he retorted immediately.

"In return," I continued, ignoring his resistance, "I promise to continue coming and to try to trust you. I promise to be there to show you I'm safe, to answer the phone to let you know I'm safe and to tell you if I feel like I'm unsafe. I will."

He was quiet for a few moments. "I really want to help you through this, Lorijane," he said. "So we'll try it. I'll see you this afternoon then?"

"I'll be there," I replied. "I promise."

*

Over the course of the next few weeks Dr. Nelson committed himself completely to my therapy. I sometimes wondered if he had any other patients because when I wasn't in his office, he was calling me several times a day just to check in, just to make sure I was still breathing. I felt like I had become an important project to him, that he'd decided I was going to be the person he saved. If he never saved anyone else, he was going to save me.

I still don't think I was telling him the whole truth. We went over Kaela's life and death in detail during our sessions. While I'd been doing it on my own before, I was now sharing my thoughts and doubts and shame and anger with him. I shared what I'd read in Kaela's journals and how I cringed at the thought that I had been the one to introduce the two of them. David's dad driving threateningly around the neighborhood and his harsh words about me. That they were lying side by side in the earth, even now, only miles away. Slowly but surely, he was allowing me to vent and working me through the stages of grief.

"Where are you right now? You're off in space somewhere at the moment, I can tell," he said one afternoon. I had trailed off and was daydreaming, my eyes unfocused. His voice brought me back, and I answered truthfully without considering whether I should lie.

"I was thinking about the ankles," I said. "They always talk about people slashing their wrists, but wouldn't the ankles work as well? It might be easier to pull off, and an ankle wound wouldn't be so obvious in the casket."

"So you want to slash your ankles?" he asked.

"Well . . . I was just thinking about it, in a general way. It's not like I have a razor blade or a knife on me or anything."

"But you do at home." I was silent when he mentioned this. "I've told you before, Lorijane, that if I fear you are an active danger to yourself, you will have to be hospitalized."

"And I told you before that if you threaten me with that, I will walk out that door and never come back." I stood up to leave. I was so mad. I thought we had covered this and come to an agreement. I was just starting to trust him and feel comfortable. Granted, I was still thinking about suicide several times a day but I hadn't actually attempted anything. I'd stepped back from that precipice I'd been playing chicken with before Philip forced me into Dr. Nelson's care. I was eating and had put on several pounds. I was brushing my hair and even taking care of my fingernails, something that seemed pointless and trivial in the dark weeks before therapy.

"They're just thoughts," I said, still poised to leave if necessary. "I don't think they have any power over me. And if I did, I would tell you."

It was a power struggle. I simply wasn't going let him put me away like that. I wasn't going to give up what little control I had left. I couldn't. I made the terms, and if he wanted honesty, it was going to be on my terms.

"Sit down, Lorijane," he said. "I think I believe you. I think you finally want to feel better." The perceptive truth of this statement struck me hard. I hadn't quite realized that for myself.

"Sit down," he continued. "That means that the real hard work is about to begin."

## Chapter Fifteen

The first part of my work with Dr. Nelson was what he called grief therapy, focusing solely on the loss of my daughter Kaela. Before we began, I would have said that I had gone over and over her death in the eight months since she died, that I had completely confronted it, but I was very wrong on that count. I had obsessed over it, yes, but instead of even attempting to come to terms with her loss, I had been beating myself up with the event like a blunt weapon.

From my experience, there was not a lot of literature out there about how to deal with suicide that I found especially helpful. It dealt in platitudes, like the idea that time heals all wounds. No one blatantly came out and said what I was coming to realize: that suicide was always going to be an open wound, and that the healing process became instead, how to live with the wound, how to live around it.

For one, other types of death had recognizable causes. In a car accident, a parent can blame drunk driving, speeding, faulty safety equipment in the car, the weather, or any number of other factors that directly led to the tragic death of their child. When a child dies due to disease, they may curse the powerlessness of modern medicine. Even if they are murdered, there is someone to blame, something tangible to point to. That's not to say that parents who lose children to means other than suicide don't deal with their own pain and grief, I know they do. But there still is a cause and an effect, and there is some kind of emotional satisfaction that comes with that understanding . . . closure, that can be had. With suicide, there are no firm answers about cause and the only finger of blame you will point -- and I guarantee it -- is at yourself as a parent.

Even if you -- like me -- had a close relationship, and even if he or she specifically says sorry and profess love for you -- as on my answering machine, as Kaela did -- you will deal with the heavy weight of blame on top of the already difficult grief of loss.

I was only beginning to learn with Dr. Nelson how to deal with the blame and pain when I received a call from the police department, from one of the detectives who had worked on Kaela's case. He told me that two young girls had committed suicide. The two teenage girls had fallen in love and couldn't bear the thought of telling their parents and the wider world that they were gay. Instead, they decided to die together as lovers, much as David and Kaela had.

"I wanted to know if you'd be willing to talk to one of their mothers who is having a difficult time with all of it," the detective said. "I think it would help her to talk to someone else who has experienced something similar."

The phone was shaking in my hand, as was my voice. I was so very fragile in discussing the way I was feeling and reacting to my daughter's death. I knew that I wasn't up to the task . . . of not only talking about my pain, but also sharing in someone else's.

"That's very noble of you, officer," I replied. "But I don't think I'm the person to ask. I don't think I could be much help to her at all, seeing that I'm not handling myself that well either."

He was considerate about the refusal, thanking me anyway. But before he got off the phone, he added, "So I noticed that you haven't yet picked up your daughter's death certificate. I just wanted to remind you about that, in case you forgot."

"I have not forgotten," I snipped. "Does it still read *suicide* as cause of death?"

"Yes."

"Well, I know it's not really that simple," I said, "and until the certificate reflects that, I don't want it in my possession."

I hung up.

I was tired of people treating me in this way, as a character in some tragic story they read about in the paper and who they thought they understood. After hearing my tale, they hug their own families tighter, happy they're not in the same position, and they pity me. Pity, I found, is very far from the realm of empathy. Then again, some people would just rather that you and our tragic story fade away, unseen and unheard, as was the case with Kaela's former school, Broad Run High.

Months after her death, I had gone to great pains to set up a scholarship in Kaela's name to give to the school, to help out another teenager as they moved on to college and the next step in their lives. As Kaela never would, I grieved. I thought it was a fitting memorial for my daughter, and I also thought that taking measurable actions like that might help me along in my recovery, which I felt like was beginning to happen with the help of Dr. Nelson. First, the principal said no. In addition to Kaela and David, the school district had seen several more students commit suicide over the past few years. There were the two lesbian girls, a young boy who died rather than tell his parents some trouble he got into and, perhaps saddest, a 12-year-old kid who suffered from bullying. The school already had a bad reputation regarding suicide, the principal said to me. The last thing they wanted was to have a scholarship in honor of one of the victims of what they preferred to keep quiet.

I took the issue to the superintendent and eventually argued the case in front of the school board. In both cases, I found that the school would much rather ignore the problem than confront the uncomfortable issue of suicide with their students and with the community. And they wanted to bury Kaela's memory in the community consciousness along with it. My point was that obviously the school had a problem and therefore the way to prevent the continuation or worsening of the problem of teen suicide at the school was to confront it. Nonetheless, they actually refused to accept the money, refused to award it to a deserving child so they could avoid worsening their reputation.

With that money still in hand, I tried to do the next best thing and donated the funds to the Broad Run Guidance Department for more suicide prevention training for their counselors.

Still I was disappointed. I had set out to do something concrete in my daughter's name in order to feel like I was taking steps in my own recovery. In the end, I felt like my efforts were thwarted at every turn and that the world just didn't want to deal with me, that the world would rather take my sorry story and my sorry self and sweep us under the rug. It seemed like unless I totally stopped taking Kaela's death so personally -- or stopped "playing the victim," as some people made me feel I was -- no one was going to take me seriously or treat me as a normal person again with something to offer.

But I wasn't playing the victim. I was just *being*. Or trying to.

Another concrete step I tried to take was with the American Foundation for Suicide Prevention. They had gotten involved with our family soon after Kaela's death thanks to a referral, but while I was suicidal, I paid them little attention. They sent books and pamphlets, but I was in no mood to read them. That literature talked about ways to feel better, and I hadn't wanted to feel better at that point. I wanted to wallow. More importantly, I hadn't come to terms with the fact that there was something wrong with me that could be fixed, or that someone out there might be able to help me fix it. It was only once I started taking baby steps toward recovery that I took a second look at the AFSP and its "feel better" literature.

I was given an AFSP survivor's pin to wear on my clothing if I wished, and at first I balked at the title of "survivor." It seemed too much like the word victim. But a local representative of the group explained to me that just like someone who has been in a train wreck and survived, I had been in an emotional train wreck and survived. My world had been turned upside down and I was facing a long road of recovery, and therefore, survivor was an apt description.

I sometimes could wear that pin, and I sometimes couldn't. Part of me was still ashamed that I was surviving, that I wasn't with my daughter and my father in the place they were now. Or I wished that Kaela could be the one wearing the pin while I was the one gone. Even though they did their best to be compassionate and helpful, I knew that the people at the AFSP simply did not understand my particular struggle. Rather than healing from one suicide or even multiple suicides, I was handling a search inside myself for a perhaps hereditary suicide gene, something both shameful and inevitable. Calling myself a survivor didn't exactly make me feel proud.

I also participated in and helped organize one of the Foundation's "Out of the Darkness" walks, fundraising events to honor the deceased by suicide and to assist their families and friends. I threw myself into the event, dedicating what energy I was regaining, completely, and it was a success. I seemed at a minor impasse. I was feeling better, but I wasn't feeling anywhere near fine or, even further away, good. It's as if I had been climbing a steep mountain in my quest to get my life back on track. The peak of the hill seemed impossibly high, and I was exhausted with the effort to reach it. But the moment I sat down to enjoy the view, I saw that the real summit was still twice as high as the first above me, the trail winding away into the clouds. I had come so far, in a way, but the way ahead was as daunting as ever.

Yes, I had begun to re-enter life in minor ways. Not only was I taking care of myself, but my thoughts were no longer taking up all of my time and energy. I was thinking about how nice it would be to get out of the house, take a vacation or even get a full-time job again. I didn't know if I was steady enough yet, but the thought was there encouraging me to continue. At the same time, my grief and pain wasn't going away and I still had that switch inside tempting me turn off the lights forever, tempting me toward the easy way out.

One of the other concrete steps that Dr. Nelson suggested for these times when my dark waves of emotion started to rise again was to carry around two pictures in my wallet: one of my daughter Niki and one of my dad. I suppose it turned my attention away from Kaela, reminding me that there were other important people in my life that I loved, one that was still here with me, if out of the nest and doing her own thing most of the time. Dr. Nelson had told me to think of those photos -- and the people in them -- like a life raft, to let them buoy me up. I did as he said, keeping them with me and pulling them out during moments of extreme pain.

During this tentative time, Dr. Nelson changed practices and moved into a different clinic facility in a different location, one where it just turned out that I had to drive by Broad Run High School each and every time I went for sessions. It's a tribute to the grief therapy that Dr. Nelson had been working on with me that I was able to complete the task at all.

Just the sight of the school was so painful to me, both because it reminded me of Kaela and all her wasted potential and also because of their somewhat callous treatment of me about the scholarship after her death. It was like turning the corner on a big black cloud with a fierce magnetic pull. It dragged down my spirits to the point where it was almost a physical blow. The school literally made me want to close my eyes and disappear, to disappear the events of the past and the pain I still carried around. One probably shouldn't close eyes while driving, however.

Over time, however, Dr. Nelson and I had confronted my pain and the places and things that triggered it. Instead of promising me the pure relief of time or the gradual fading of pain, Dr. Nelson had forced me to understand that a pain so traumatic would never fully disappear and that I needed to stop expecting it to -- or berating myself when it didn't magically go away. It was going to be there as long as I was, so if I wanted to continue putting one foot in front of the other in life, I needed to acknowledge the pain and be able to turn and confront it.

The biggest revelation was that even though I had to pull it from deep down within me, I had the strength to do so. At least with little things, at least sometimes, but even that was revelatory.

The school was just one small example. If it wasn't the actual vision and thought and history of that school in my head, if I replaced that with the thought of something else, I could handle it. I might not relish driving past the spot, but I could manage it if I replaced that triggering thought with something that was innocuous.

For the trigger of the school, for instance, I did what the Ghostbusters did in their first movie and thought of something that didn't seem at all scary: the Stay Puff

Marshmallow Man. It may sound silly, and at first, it felt that way to me, too. Picturing a big, white and puffy cartoon character, however, reminded me that the school was only an object, just like the Marshmallow Man. It was only a thing in the world that I had to see and interact with in daily life, and how I chose to react to it was up to me. The school wasn't hurting me; I was letting the school hurt me without even throwing up a defensive stance.

Gradually, through such small techniques, I found myself able to see my emotional pain as something that I couldn't avoid feeling, but was able to turn toward and face, and it changed my reaction to it. The negative emotion doesn't necessarily lead to the negative action.

I could employ the same technique to the constant questions that suicide survivors face. *Why did she do it? What could I have done? What was wrong? What could have stopped her? Is this my fault?* Instead of allowing the questions to back mc into a corner where they could overwhelm my defenses to the point that I could not function, I had to hear the questions, recognize that they were valid, but also understand that they would never and could never be answered. They would hang around my head for the rest of my life no matter what I did, so I was forced to find a way to coexist with those questions. It wasn't easy, but it did allow me to take baby steps forward.

Certainly it was a valuable trick, but in the end, it did still feel like a trick to me, a crutch to get me by for now. But people who were fully healed didn't need crutches. I still felt broken, like a toy glued together but not as good as new. In fact, I wondered when I'd ever felt really whole and unbroken and I continued to think of whether my powerful genetics -- which might be bent toward self destruction -- could rear their ugly head in the future. I didn't think that the Marshmallow Man or any other cartoon character would be enough for me to stand and fight against the forces of darkness I still felt roiling inside of me.

I brought up the subject with Dr. Nelson in our therapy sessions. He was still as dedicated and vigilant as ever about keeping track of my safety. I had kept my promise about being honest with him, so while he knew I wasn't sneaking down to the car in the middle of the night, he also knew that I struggled many times a day with feelings of worthlessness and hopelessness.

"I hear what you're feeling, and I think that you're right. I think we are missing something as yet," he said. "We've been talking a lot about Kaela, her death, and how to cope with that loss, but we've only taken the most cursory glances back into your life further, before the kids, when you were a kid yourself. Even though a similar incident happened in your childhood, you don't seem to like to talk about it. Why do you think that is?"

"It was so long ago," I replied. "Besides, like I told you, I was encouraged to bottle that stuff up to the point that it doesn't seem right to talk about it, or sometimes even to think about it."

"Even so, I don't think we can ignore the fact that not only did your childhood affect you deeply – it's impossible it didn't, really -- but that there are connections between your childhood and your situation today," he said. "I think we should confront some of these things if you really want to move forward."

It seemed to me a dangerous proposition, especially considering the fact that he called it the technical term "confrontational therapy." Confrontation didn't sound like fun, but it also seemed to be the only way to continue forward up this second peak I had seen after reaching the false summit of my initial recovery.

I agreed. Perhaps not enthusiastically. I did feel a small glimmer of hope that this route might lead toward recovery, but that was balanced with a huge weight of fear, made heavier with the emotional baggage of my childhood.

*

The first bit of confrontation Dr. Nelson employed regarded the issue of my mother, Joan.

"And why don't you want to call her your mother, or Mom?" he asked me. "Why call her by her first name?"

"Well, it's not like she was very much of a mother to me. I honestly consider Ruby my mother," I said. "At times, it seemed Joan might just up and kill me on the spot, and she told me so many times that I should never have been born in the first place."

I had started talking about the subject of Joan by simply saying she was abusive, but gradually the memories came out of me in fits and starts. There were the large abuses like the skillet to the back of my brother's head and the strap across my bare bottom. There were the slaps, black eyes and fat lips. The incidents that caused the most shock and physical pain came out first. Then I started to recall and relate the smaller things, like alum in the mouth and the Lava soap.

Because I'd never before tried to delve into that part of my life in depth, I had no idea that my memory was so strange and spotty. Dr. Nelson explained to me that was a perfectly normal reaction to trauma, to repress and mix up memories, or to remember different parts of memories at different times. When the brain reacts to trauma, it sometimes allows only a certain slice of our memories to be accessible at any one time as a self-preservation measure. Remembering it all at once would be overwhelming. Dr. Nelson compared it to the concept of bandwidth, that my mind might be capable of handling only a certain amount of traumatic information. Sometimes things got confused or lost when I was trying to remember too much. That's why he probed and confronted me in so many different ways, to stir up new places in my memory during each session so we'd eventually see the larger picture that was obscured even from me.

He asked me to talk in greater detail about Joan's character and habits, and that dredged up thoughts about how she hated people to get too close to her realm of personal space and how she needed the home to be her ordered kingdom, with everything in place and clean according to her rules. I even remembered her hatred of bodily odors and how we had to run outside to relieve ourselves or if we felt sick and were about to vomit.

"You are quite turned off by vomit, too, aren't you?" he probed.

"Well, yeah," I answered, getting defensive. "It's not exactly a pleasant thing to anyone, but I'm not going to go around slapping a child or hurting them in any way just because they vomit."

"Of course not, but you have to see that your mother displayed obsessive behavior very similar to your own? To a much more serious degree in many ways, however."

I crossed my arms in anger, not responding.

"I'm not saying she was in any way justified for her violence toward you or your siblings," he continued. "Nonetheless, that obsessive behavior is something that's there and that you should process."

"I feel like you're making excuses for her violence."

"Never. No one is justified in striking a child," he said. "Tell me, do you think you believed or still believe the things that Joan said about you and the other kids? That you were worthless and unwanted and somehow bad?"

I had to think about this for a while. As a kid, such statements were such a part of everyday family life that I rarely stopped to think about their truth or the effect they had on me. I had to look back at the child I was and try to remember how she thought about herself, what she thought was her self worth.

"I never was a confident kid. I really thought that she hated me, and I still do on that count. I suppose she made me feel as if no one wanted me around and everyone was against me, even the nuns and teachers who were supposed to help. You feel a little like a leper or an outcast, and you never feel you can tell anyone the whole truth about who you are, or they'd definitely not like you," I said. "Her words made me feel that I was totally on my own, that I couldn't count on anyone in this world -- except Dad."

I thought for another minute, then added, "And I never believed that Dad attacking her was the fault of us kids. I could never believe that."

"That's very interesting," Dr. Nelson replied. "But you have to admit that no one is wholly evil, like it seems like your mother is in your mind and memory. Hate and fear can take up a lot of mental energy, you know, and they give the memory of that person a lot of power to use against us."

He tapped on his notepad. "Do you think there might have been any more to your mother that you didn't know about?"

It was a coincidence that he asked, because strangely enough, I had just found a big source of new information about Joan that I was previously unaware of. Through the tangled web of connections that is the social media, perhaps through Facebook, some member of the family had just mentioned that my mother had written a book. At first, I thought perhaps the book would talk about my childhood and the shooting. After all, those events would have to make up one of the most dramatic parts of anyone's life, including Joan's. Instead, she had gone further back in time to her own growing up, writing a book called "Tales from the Depression" – using her married name from her second husband.

I tracked down a copy, though it was relatively difficult to find, since it was an Internet self-published memoir. For someone who had at least consciously cut her mother out of her life and claimed that her mother no longer had any effect on her, I guess I was more eager to read it than I might have admitted. It was written in a disjointed and amateurish way, but the story was clear enough as I read it. In my opinion, it was a "poor me" type of sob story written to make others pity Joan, and perhaps even forgive her sins.

She began by talking about that old house she'd shown me growing up where her family used to live. There were more kids than her parents knew what to do with and a few unlucky ones they buried along the way, too. She wrote a great deal about the effects of the Depression on her family, the scarcity of food and the bed bugs that tormented them in the few mattresses they all shared. Maybe she was trying to relate how they had no toys to play with.

"So when you or Mike took an extra stale, day-old cookie or some chips from the kitchen counter, what do you think that made your mother think?" asked Dr. Nelson, again confronting me in uncomfortable ways.

"I know what you're doing," I said. "You want me to say that she reacted so extremely because she was always in the mindset that food was scarce, that we could fall to having absolutely nothing because of something silly like that. That she beat us because she had a poor, sad childhood."

"It is silly that one cookie or something could cause family-wide hunger, but is it possible she thought that way?"

"I suppose, but . . ."

"And is it possible that because she was a little OCD in her housecleaning -- like you, remember -- that could also have been a trigger about her own traumatic past?"

I was silent, seething at this line of thought, that the therapist that was supposed to help me was forcing me into this absolutely wrong direction.

"As for her obsession with religious purity, do you think it's possible that stemmed from the same source? She might have thought of you kids as the evidence of her own filthiness and sin."

"She was the one who called all of us sinners!"

"All from the same source: a driving need for purity."

"Why are you trying to make me like her?!" I finally lost my temper and yelled, standing up from the sofa to do so. Even the white-noise machines would have had a hard time keeping that yell from not echoing down the hall. I stood there for a while staring daggers at Dr. Nelson, my shoulders heaving with each breath, but he just stared calmly back with his legs casually crossed.

After he judged I'd calmed down, he motioned for me to sit.

"I'm not trying to make you like her, Lorijane. With the things she did to you, of course you will never like her," he said. "Instead, don't you see that what I'm trying to make you see is that it's actually all about you, about that little girl who suffered at her hands?"

I shook my head.

"These things we're talking about, it means she's only a human, a poor, sad and flawed human," he said. "It means that you didn't do anything to deserve it, that it's not your fault. The way she made you feel, that was at least partially her issues coming down on your head."

I was silent for a long moment, letting that thought sink in. *Did I -- do I -- really think that the way I was treated in my childhood was my fault? Has that really affected how I've felt about myself my whole life?* I had never thought about my life from that perspective before, but it was true that my mother told me I was wild, uncontrollable, worthless, unwanted and inherently evil down to the bone. It was true that I believed I was uncontrollable, because my OCD proved that I imposed order to control myself and my life. It was true that I often felt unlovable to anyone, even myself, and that I felt my decline and death was inevitable due to some evil in me beyond my control.

If it was true that my mother had continued to impact everything I did and everything I was in subtle ways, it means my usual way of looking at myself and looking at my childhood was wrong. It wasn't my fault. Her behavior and her words had nothing to do with me, only with herself. In some ways, that made me hate her all the more, that she put me and my siblings and Dad through such hell purely because of her own personality, whims and inner demons. But mostly, I just felt relieved.

*I was a normal kid and I deserved a normal childhood,* I thought. *Therefore, I'm a normal person and I deserve a normal life.*

"Remember, you cannot control what happens to you," said Dr. Nelson. "You can only control how you behave in response."

I was lost in my new train of thought, but I nodded. "I'm going to need some time to think about all of this," I said.

## Chapter Sixteen

If it was his goal to make me an angrier person, Dr. Nelson was definitely succeeding. I banged the door to his office open, sending it bouncing off the doorstopper on the wall, and huffed over to his couch with my arms already defensively crossed.

"All right," I said. "Let's get this over with."

He regarded me with a bemused expression. "And who are you?" he questioned. "Lorijane, is that Lorijane?"

"Funny," I replied, waving my hand to show him I was ready to get on with it. He smiled and obliged me.

"So I think it's about time that we talked some about your father then," said Dr. Nelson as we continued on our journey of therapy.

It really was beginning to feel like a journey -- a long road trip in a confined space where, even if you really like and respect your traveling companion, you begin to feel the need to strangle him, too. That was sometimes how I felt about Dr. Nelson, whom I pictured dangling a carrot in front of me but carrying a pointy fire iron behind, always sharply pushing me forward toward the destination.

At least I was thinking that there was a destination somewhere in sight. That alone kept me from throttling my talented therapist.

"What about Dad? He wasn't really a problem. I loved Dad. Dad was more like he was my cool big brother or we were pals, hanging around together for fun rather than him teaching me life lessons and things like that. We joked around, and he teased me with all those nicknames. My time with him was some of the only bright patches of my whole childhood. I loved him very much."

Dr. Nelson pierced me with his dark eyes, trying to gauge how I was going to react to what he was going to say. I could tell.

"But it's true that because of Dad, you were often very hurt, right?" he asked.

"What do you mean?"

"Well, for one, there were a lot of accidents. A screwdriver went through your leg. You rolled out of a moving truck that was speeding too fast." It's like he was ticking these things off on his fingers.

"Like you said, those were accidents," I replied. "It doesn't mean he didn't love me. I mean, nothing was as safety-oriented back then as it is today. Michelle rode around in the back of a car in something like a play pen, not a car seat, just rolling around back there. Kids made potato guns and rode bikes without helmets."

"But he also allowed your mother to beat you."

The statement hung in the air between us. There was no way for me to deny it was true, of course. He had been there for years while Joan carried on her campaign of terror, and though he never allowed it in his presence, he was unable or unwilling to stop it from continuing in his absence.

"He was out of the house. When he wasn't at work, he was out working in his garage, trying to make money," I said. "He always told her to stop."

My throat was getting tight, and no more words would come out.

"He couldn't stop her?" Dr. Nelson asked. I nodded. "Or was it that he wasn't willing to stop her? Was it that he didn't do enough to stop her?"

"That's not fair!"

"Well, look at it this way," he continued. "If someone was beating your child, what would you do to them? What would you do to make them stop hurting your child?"

"I'd murder them," I growled. "I'd do anything."

My Mama Bear hackles were definitely raised at the thought of either one of my two beautiful daughters suffering any type of physical abuse. To me, they would always be tiny creatures with tiny fingers curled into fists, wrapped in hospital blankets and yawning in my arms on the days they were born. So fragile, so innocent. I thought I could literally murder someone who even attempted to do to a child of mine what had been done to me.

I stopped to think about the connection Dr. Nelson was trying to get me to make.

"Are you saying that he didn't mind me getting hurt, or even that he wanted me to continue being hurt?" I demanded.

"No, not really," he replied. "I think that your dad genuinely loved you. You know that. You felt it, and that's why you gravitated toward his presence. It's also why you've built him up to be such a shining knight in your mind's eye. As you said, the one bright spot of your childhood."

I thought about the trips in his old truck to get ice cream on summer evenings, of curling up in his lap to watch television or for me to read him the newspaper. His perfectly combed, shiny hair, twinkling eyes and mischievous smile flashed before my eyes. I could remember the sound of his truck on the gravel of the drive and the way I'd fly out the front door and into his arms.

But then I thought about the bruises and black eyes I'd show him, that he'd shake his head and ask what I had done to get Joan so worked up this time, like it was a long-running joke. He'd come into the kitchen with a scowl on his face sometimes and yell, telling Joan to cut it out already, but then she'd offer a flippant remark and he'd sit down to eat, considering his work done. That last night in the truck, what had he said? *"I want you to know that everything is going to be fine now. Everything is going to be better for you and your sister from now on."*

And then he was dead.

"He said he was going to change it, that last night," I said.

"Yes, I think that evening weighs on you, doesn't it?"

"I've always wondered if I had done something different or if I'd said something . . ." My voice was almost a whisper by now. "There must have been something I could have done that would have changed his mind about what he was going to do. Some way of warning him not to . . . to stop him."

"You were thirteen," he said. "And even if you weren't, no one can predict the future. How could you have known what was going to happen next? He had no history of doing anything so violent or spontaneous as shooting your mother and himself. Like you've often said -- and beat yourself up about I might add -- he in no way met the typical profile of someone about to commit suicide."

I was silent for a while, my hands twisting around each other in my lap.

"But to shift the subject, do you think he planned on committing suicide that day? Was that the plan going in?"

I shook my head. "Of course I can't know for sure, but I don't think so. That's my opinion, at least," I said. "I think that something went wrong in his plan, or maybe he hadn't really planned what he was going to do at all."

"But there is a moment of choice," Dr. Nelson added. "You have more experience than almost anyone with that moment where you make up your mind to commit suicide, when you make an active move to end yourself, erase your presence and consciousness. What do you think was going on in your dad's head? What was he thinking?"

"He was so proud," I said with a sad smile. "I don't think he could bear to face the consequences of what he'd just done. Going to jail, a trial, people knowing about all our dirty laundry and gossiping."

"So it wasn't you that he was thinking about?"

I looked up at him, rather startled.

"Well," he continued, "I think it would be only rational that if you're thinking of the consequences, the thought of your children and family, the people you'd be leaving behind, would definitely be of the utmost consideration. Don't you think?"

"Yes. I . . . I don't know," I said, thinking back to my own experiences playing chicken with that moment in the recent past, toying with the switch, as I thought of it. First and foremost on my mind had been the intensity of my own pain and self-hatred, that I wanted to wipe myself off the face of the earth. There was the feeling of freedom at discovering I had that power, that I had power over this most all-encompassing matter of life and death. There was the elation. On the other side of the coin, there was my fear of blood and vomit and mess, of appearing wounded or ugly in my casket. Silly, but true. Down there on the totem pole, there was the thought of Niki, my beloved daughter; but if I was being honest with myself, the rest of the jumble came first and was more intense.

"Do you think he thought about you at all?" Dr. Nelson asked. I didn't respond. "I mean, you and especially Michelle were still so very young. He was going to be leaving you with a physically and verbally abusive mother -- "

"He could have thought she was dead, or dying!"

"Okay. But he had some sort of rift with his family. He hated all of her family," he said. "He had to have known that the likely scenario would be the one that actually unfolded: you being dumped into an uncaring foster system, cut off from everyone and everything you knew. I mean, it's kind of obvious if you give it even the slightest thought."

"It all happened so fast, I'm sure. Firing off the shots. Turning the gun around . . . Shooting, cocking, turning it back around, shooting again . . . But the moments are so unreal and drawn out so long. He must have thought of me, of us kids. He had to have. Didn't he?"

Dr. Nelson shrugged. "What do you think?"

I thought about those unreal, drawn-out moments of my own when I was only a hairsbreadth away from killing myself. The only person I was really thinking about was me. My pain. My past. My life. My thoughts. My loss.

"Perhaps the question shouldn't be if he thought of you," he went on. "After all, we can't always control our own thoughts. Perhaps the real question is, should he have?"

My eyes snapped closed and my face collapsed with the pressure of a building sob. Tears were already coursing down my cheeks, and I hunched over into myself, doing my best to curl up into as small a speck as possible. Dr. Nelson had his hand on my shoulder and promptly provided a whole box off tissues to stem the tide of waterworks that I had become.

It was as if my father had died and left me all alone in that world just at that moment, not decades before. Most of my life I had been stunned and hurt at the tragedy that unfolded the day I lost my father, but never before had I put the pieces together in such a way that I made him the bad guy. The incident had been something that happened, but now I saw that it was something that was done to me. Done to me by the father I had idolized to the point of saintliness. It hurt. It broke my heart. The overwhelming selfishness of his act, thinking only of himself and tossing me and Michelle out the window as if we were of no consequence.

Back came the anger that had been growing over the last weeks and months of therapy, rage flooding through my veins like adrenaline. After a few sobbing moments, it vaporized my tears and I had it together enough to finally answer his question.

"Yes," I said firmly, insistently. "Yes, he should have."

"And?" Dr. Nelson prodded.

"So should I."

*

After that breakthrough, Dr. Nelson reminded me about the photos he'd had me carry with me for the last few weeks, one of Niki -- young, smiling and holding a friend's adorable little dog -- and one of Dad -- old-fashioned and sepia-toned. When I had begun carrying around the pictures, I had thought that Dr. Nelson meant them to be an anchor for me, the people I loved most acting like a tether to keep me connected to the physical world and to life itself. Certainly, they'd served that purpose, reminding me that I had love in my life.

Now that I understood myself from a different perspective, however, the photographs took on increased meaning as I stared at them. In my left hand was Dad, the man who had loved me, that I knew for sure. But he was also a man with faults, including a lack of temerity to insist upon my safety and a selfish need for escape that had thrown me into awful circumstances, both in the real world and mentally. In my right hand was my daughter Niki. We were perhaps not as close as Kaela and I had been. Niki was always one to go her own way in the world and damn the consequences. But this was the girl to whom I would not do the same, with whom I would not repeat history. I had to live with the never-ending cycle of questions about two different suicides in my life and fight that death match of blame. If I committed suicide, would it be Niki's fault? Of course not. But if I did, she would ask herself every day and every minute if it was, and did I want that? Of course not.

These two photographs were the key to stopping the cycle: here, now, and for good.

It was the anger that broke through to me in the end, and it had taken a long time for Dr. Nelson to work me up to that anger, coaxing me toward it without me seeing it was part of the master plan. I can't believe what I put him through during that period and think perhaps he's the one that should be nominated for sainthood. He'd broken through every barrier and dove to the bottom of an ocean of grief to find where I'd hidden the real Lorijane and then dragged her back to the surface kicking and screaming. It definitely took a little time for resolution afterward to help me put all that I had learned into perspective.

"If Dad had wanted me, he would have stayed and fought for me," I said. "That's how I see it. Being connected with other people and being alive in general takes work, and in the end, it's selfish not to stand tall and shoulder that work." I sighed. "It all comes back to Kaela's wisdom in the end, doesn't it? It all comes back to that homelessness project when she spoke about people just dropping out of life."

"That's the first time you've smiled thinking about Kaela in a while," Dr. Nelson noted. "It's nice to see. It's also nice to see that while you've discovered anger, you're not angry with Kaela. Why is that, you think?"

I shook my head. "I know how tempting it is to give in to the darkness," I explained. "And she was so young and impressionable. I don't think she knew how to turn away, to say, 'I cannot control what happens to me. I can only control how I react to it.'"

It was his turn to smile, hearing his words spoken back to him.

I could spout the words, of course, but I knew I wasn't completely healed. The holidays had just passed, a stressful time for anyone, but especially for a family celebrating for the first time without a child. I had ups and downs. But more importantly, I was moving forward. I had moved ahead and started divorce proceedings with Philip, who turned out to be a bigger jerk than I had ever imagined. He had been embezzling money from our consulting company and doing other questionable things while I had been too ill to pay attention. I had reconnected with Niki, telling her that she and I were in this thing called life together, that we were family. We both had suffered great loss, but we needed to pull together in order to make it through, together. I had gotten an apartment of my own in order to move out of the house in which my daughter died. I had a new bank account, and I was looking for work again. It was as if the anger ignited me.

"So how is the suicide ideation then?" Dr. Nelson asked me. "What do you think about that dark time now that you look back on it from where you are now?"

"I got so close sometimes that it scares me," I admitted. "It was such a strong force, and it also scares me that I know that force is still inside of me, that it's not been destroyed. When I think about some of the close calls . . . I don't know. I guess I'm glad that my obsessive nature made me pull back from so much. It might have saved me."

"I don't know about that," he said. "You may have wanted to escape, but deep down, you didn't want to die. Deep down you had reservations that manifested in that excuse about messes. Not that you weren't honestly concerned about the mess, but that was your sub-consciousness' way of giving you a way out, a way of pulling back. Your brain gave you an out."

"Hmm," I said, wondering about that.

"How's Niki?" he asked, wrapping up our session with a little casual talk.

I had to smile. "She's doing great," I said, talking about how she was faring after childbirth. Taking after her mother, she'd gotten pregnant unmarried and was going to be a single mom, at least for the foreseeable future. I thought it would work out okay, though, because the child's grandma was going to be around for a long time and be very involved. "It looks like my first grandchild might be as wild as her mother with the way she cries, though. She might just give her a run for her money."

I've talked a lot with Niki about the recovery process, wanting her to learn a little from what I had struggled to find out. I have never outright told her about her photo, however, the one I carried around with me, close to my heart. The one that saved my life.

## Epilogue

I don't want to pretend that I have any superhuman insight into recovery from being suicidal. I don't believe that there is any one way in which to find yourself and your reason for living again. There are many different methods to meet the needs of all sorts of different people, and I would never presume to advise someone which would be the best for their particular history, personality and circumstances.

Instead, I have written down my story for other reasons. First of all, it's something that I do for myself. It helps me make sense of my own experience as I piece it together for others, seeing the story as if from the outside instead of imprisoned within it. I've found the perspective to be powerful and liberating, an antidote to what I once felt and still struggle with regarding the value of my life and my self-worth.

For readers, however, I wanted to provide a story that perhaps would have helped me during my darkest days, a book that doesn't make promises or convey empty platitudes, but instead speaks honestly and openly about the subject of suicide. I wanted to tell you from the inside the thoughts and emotions and motivations of someone who has come so close to causing their own death that they could have reached out to touch the other side.

There are thousands of other people like me. We are real people. We are out there in the world, thinking we're completely alone or entirely abnormal. And that's just not the case.

The mindset of someone contemplating suicide cannot be deemed "normal" by any stretch of the imagination. It's a dangerous state of mind, and one that does need changing. However, feeling suicidal is normal in certain circumstances, especially when faced with extreme tragedy. It happens to all sorts of people all over the world every day, but since they're squirreled away battling their own misery, it's difficult to see that it happens to someone outside yourself. You feel alone. You feel that no one on earth could possibly have felt this kind of pain before, that no one would understand.

I want to say that I do. I both sympathize and empathize as no one untouched with suicide can, and I know that there is a great deal of comfort to be found just in the revelation that you are not alone, not by a long shot. What you feel is not healthy and you need to get help in order to turn your life back into healthy territory -- I should have sought help long before I did -- but it can be done. It's not exactly like I was the easiest case, the kind that jumps right on the bandwagon, saying, "I can change! I can get better!" I had to be pushed, pulled and prodded back into the world of life, but I found a way. Therefore, the way that you're feeling *can* improve and it is possible to come back from the brink of suicide.

I'm living proof. *Living* being the operative word.

I'm also not writing to paint a rosy little picture about recovering from either the suicide of a loved one or your own brushes with suicide. I would be outright lying, and personally, I found that sunshiny lies of that nature did more harm to me than good when I was deep in depression. For me, the biggest breakthrough was the realization that recovery was incredibly, unbelievably difficult -- but that it was possible. Rather than being buried alive, it was like instead finding myself only stuck at the bottom of a very deep well: a very unpleasant place to be, certainly, but with fresh air and blue sky in sight at the top of the climb.

As opposed to other forms of tragedy, the unique grief caused by suicide will never go away. It's absolutely crucial that you can accept that. The feelings of guilt can be overwhelming, but because the questions you can't help but ask after suicide can never be answered to your satisfaction, you will never stop asking them. They will follow you around for the rest of your days in the form of emotional baggage. However, it is possible that by accepting their presence and learning to live around them, those questions can one day become merely rhetorical and you can accept their open-ended nature.

The other thing that will always be a constant in the life of someone effected by suicide is the wealth of triggers you'll find around you in everyday life, stumbling over them when you least expect it. I've mentioned in particular Kaela's school and the sight of kids playing on playgrounds as triggers for me, but it's not always so obvious. In casual conversation, you will hear people say formerly innocuous phrases like "I could just die" or "I'm going to kill him," and it's difficult not to either burst into tears or rage at the speaker for the insensitivity. Whereas others may think about such things as colorful figures of speech, experience with suicide can transform such innocent words, making them seem real and flaring up your dormant pain and bitter loss.

Other people might think nothing of, during a boring social situation, putting their thumb and forefinger to their temple in the shape of a gun and pulling the trigger. For me, having seen firsthand my daughter's gunshot wound to the head, such a thing will never be all in good fun and I often have to calm myself in order to deal with such situations. Sometimes I still don't handle them well, either causing myself pain or inflicting pain upon someone who didn't mean me any harm.

Even so, I'm not afraid in such situations to bring up the subject and talk about the unknown insensitivity of such things other people just take for granted. I think talking about it educates other people about an issue that's nearly always just swept under the rug.

For instance, I once wrote an email to a local radio station whose morning deejays said something terribly insensitive. Speaking about something that happened in the news, she'd said if the same thing had happened to her, "Well, you might as well shoot me now." When I wrote, I made a point to say that I was a survivor of gun violence and, whether they were aware of it or not, there's likely hundreds of other such survivors or victims listening to their station every day. No one would feel comfortable making jokes about leukemia or cancer or other things that cause death, therefore, is it really okay to make light of shooting deaths and gun violence?

Because I'd brought up the subject in an open and calm matter and am not just another anti-gun activist, but a person who attempts to live with the aftermath of a real tragedy, the response I got was surprisingly apologetic and kind. They actually thanked me for bringing the matter to their attention, and I felt relieved that there was at least one person whose eyes had been opened to the fact that murder and suicide are no laughing matters and that there are victims and survivors of such violence walking the streets every day.

Whether or not the propensity to suicide is hereditary is a controversial subject in the psychiatric community. There are mental health professionals who argue both sides of the question. It is true that many mental health disorders are passed down through family genes and that the vast majority of people who commit suicide are suffering from a mental disorder. As for myself, I believe it. I've almost physically felt the ability to take my own life inside myself -- that inner switch that I don't believe most people possess -- and so I can't help but think that it must be true.

And so I worry. I worry about my siblings and about Niki and about my grandchildren. I'm terrified every day not only that I could fall back into the dark place I've experienced, but also that I will lose the people I love. I worry not only that they might one day suffer from what I have, but I also worry about their deaths in general terms, from car accidents or cancer or any other cause. I hold them tight to me and love them fiercely. I also make fervent efforts to reach out and educate them, to talk openly and honestly about suicide and its aftermath so as not to cause them to bottle up and internalize grief in the same way that I did.

And so I find myself here, writing a book about life, about surviving my own survival.

In my home you will find photos and sketches of Kaela, but I've made a point not to make my house a shrine to the loss of my daughter. She was a beautiful and loving girl that I had the privilege of knowing for fifteen years. It was too short a time, of course, but I wouldn't trade it or erase it for anything, even if the memory of the end of those years causes me pain. Every time I walk by one of her photos, I make a point to have a happy thought even if it's coupled with a sad one. I think about how old she would be now and what she might be studying at college. I think about bathing her as an infant or the year she took home all the awards at the 4H competition. She made a mistake, a horrible and tragic and final mistake, but she was still my sweet little daughter and I need to make sure that all my memories of her aren't clouded over with the grief of her final moments. It's a daily struggle and an ongoing process.

Recovering from the suicide of a loved one or a suicide attempt of one's own will always be an ongoing process. I conceive of it as an addiction of a sort, much like alcoholism or drug addiction. Once you open the door, or in my case, "flip the switch," you can't close the lid of Pandora's box completely. You will always know that you're capable of ending your own life and know the intense rush of adrenaline, relief and freedom that comes with it. It's a daily fight to not fall back into that fool's game.

Alcoholics Anonymous doesn't cure the disease of alcoholism; it simply gives alcoholics the tools they need to exist with their condition. So I, too, have discovered and rely upon the tools that work for me to battle my own form of addiction. I think the day I stop needing those tools will be the day that I die -- long from now, of natural causes.

I have to say thank you to my friend and therapist Dr. Nelson. When I first met him, he may have been young and inexperienced with the type of tragedy I was dealing with, but he proved himself a dedicated and clever doctor. No matter how hard of a time I gave him, he stuck by me and persevered, finally delivering me revelation and helping me find those tools that are helping me survive day to day. I couldn't have done it and I wouldn't be here today without him.

The day I left the home I had built with Philip and shared with my girls I went out on the deck where Kaela had lain in a pool of blood as she struggled to take her last breath. I remembered being out there on January 4th, the day after she had died, just walking around the blood stain thinking I couldn't step in it -- this was all that was left of my beautiful daughter. I remember it was still warm outside and as I looked down at the blood soaked planks of wood I heard the song of a wind chime. I remember looking up and seeing the chime in my neighbor's yard clanking and making sounds in the wind. At that very moment the sun caught it on its side, and clearly I could see the wind chime was made up of little hummingbirds.

# ABOUT THE AUTHOR

Lorijane Graham originally hails from the New England area though has lived in Northern Virginia for the past 20 years. She has been in the marketing /development field for 23 years and raised over $30 thousand dollars for the American Foundation for Suicide Prevention as a participant in one of their "Out of the Darkness" walks. Lorijane has one adult daughter and two grandchildren, and in her spare time enjoys designing and drawing portraits.

Made in the USA
Lexington, KY
03 April 2012